From the day Jilly Cooper first burst onto the scene with an article in *The Sunday Times Colour Magazine* she has never looked back. Her name is now a household word. She is read and discussed all over the world – her postbag bulges with approving and disapproving letters. She delights some people with her witty comments on day-to-day life, problems and people, and she irritates others beyond belief.

Here is a chance to read more of her famous collection of articles, first published in *The Sunday Times* and the *Mail on Sunday*. Her articles are full of laughter laced with good common sense. The ideal Jilly Cooper reader says: 'That's just what I've always been thinking – but I wouldn't have dared to admit it.'

Also by Jilly Cooper

IMOGEN
PRUDENCE
OCTAVIA
HARRIET
BELLA
EMILY
LISA & CO.
CLASS
JOLLY SUPER
JOLLY SUPER TOO
JOLLY SUPERLATIVE
SUPER JILLY
SUPER COOPER
INTELLIGENT AND LOYAL
VIOLETS AND VINEGAR (with Tom Hartman)

and published by Corgi Books

JOLLY MARSUPIAL

Down under and other scenes

Jilly Cooper

CORGI BOOKS

My thanks are due to the editors of *The Sunday Times* and of the *Mail on Sunday* in which most of these articles first appeared.

JOLLY MARSUPIAL

A CORGI BOOK 0 552 12359 5

Originally published in Great Britain by
Methuen London Ltd.

PRINTING HISTORY

Methuen edition published 1982
Corgi edition published 1984

Conditions of Sale

This book is set in Sabon 10/11

Corgi Books are published by
Transworld Publishers Ltd.,
Century House, 61–63 Uxbridge Road,
Ealing, London W5 5SA

Made and printed in Great Britain by
Hunt Barnard Printing Ltd., Aylesbury, Bucks.

To my father-in-law Leonard Cooper
with love and admiration

CONTENTS

Foreword

In this new volume of collected pieces which have appeared in various newspapers and magazines during the past three years, I am particularly glad to have the opportunity to publish in full what I actually wrote about my visit to Australia in 1980. Of the original fifteen-thousand-word piece, *The Sunday Times* only used 8,000 words and edited it in a way, and provided it with a headline ('Land of the Suntanned Snobs') that seriously distorted what I wanted to say. Likewise various Australian newspapers either took umbrage at what they read in *The Sunday Times* or reprinted only the sections of the original piece that suited them: as often as not they had geographical reasons for this. The net result of all these extracts was a surge of angry letters from Australians all over the world, and a great many English people, who thought I had been not only unfair but offensive.

Now I have the opportunity to put the situation to rights and even if the piece in its entirety, as originally written, does offend some people, which I suppose it is bound to, at least it is as I intended it to be. I had a wonderful time in Australia; I loved the land, the people I met, and I hope I have conveyed the enthusiasm that I felt. I think I can honestly say that they were three of the most exciting weeks of my life. Not many people on their first trip have the opportunity to visit all the major cities of that vast continent in such a short time, and I must record my gratitude to my publishers, Methuen (and Methuen of Australia) for making the whole thing possible.

Newspapers are often forced to make cuts and apply the occasional fig leaf, for reasons of space and their readers' blood pressure. At least here you read the unexpurgated version, warts, other appendages and all, of not only my Australian piece but also several other articles from the same period.

Among the other pieces included in this volume are the first two long articles on men I wrote for the new *Mail on Sunday* (here published together as 'The day of the wimp'). After thirteen and a half years I decided to leave *The Sunday Times* and seek fresh pastures. I only hope that by the time this book appears, the grass will still be as green on the other side of the fence as it seems to be at the moment.

May 1982

Down under

Pom on the run

Few people can have set out for Australia with more trepidation than I did. A week before I left I saw a programme on television called *Kerry Packer and the Poms*, which gave me a taste of the rabidly anti-English sentiment I might expect. Then a very unsunny lady from the *Melbourne Sun* came to interview me in London and asked why the hell was I going there to promote a silly book on the English class system when Australia was a classless society anyway. Finally the itinerary for the tour arrived. In ten days it included a punishing total of sixty-eight interviews with press, television and radio, three launching parties, five speeches, and 36,000 miles of flying to eight different cities, including Singapore and Hong Kong.

Arriving in Sydney at seven o'clock in the morning, however, we were met not by a shower of tins, or by a snarling Dennis Lillee bowling bumpers, but by a couple of pot-bellied health inspectors who solemnly entered the plane and sprayed us with flit.

'No wonder that fly got off at Singapore,' said my husband.

Inside the airport there was a dearth of trolleys and a plethora of beautiful suntanned girls, their faces gleaming greeny-brown like poplar leaves in spring. A kind man helped us carry our cases. A kind woman showed me where the paper towels were hidden in the Ladies. On the loo wall, someone had scribbled: 'Keep Australia Green – Have Sex with a Frog.'

Waiting like zombies in the cafeteria for our flight to Brisbane, we watched a man breakfast off chocolate milk shake and oysters. At the bar two men in blazers were drinking beer.

At Brisbane we were met by our tour organizer, a splendid Brunhilda with waist-length brown hair and a flawless skin called Elsa Petersen. True to her namesake, she behaved towards us throughout the tour like a kindly lioness with two very wayward cubs. When I grumbled that I'd never last the pace, she promptly presented me with some vitamin pills. According to the label, they were 'for use in pregnancy, alcoholism and advanced liver complaints'. This seemed somewhat drastic, but once I got over the shock of drinking neat Tizer for breakfast every morning, they worked wonders. All Australians live on vitamin pills.

First impressions of Brisbane were hazy: trees with great grey trunks shaped like Indian clubs; women with parasols; brilliant dogs balancing on the top of moving cars and open lorries, who barked when the lights went green; houses perched on stilts, with steps up to the front door; and balconies fretted at the top and bottom like lace Victorian Christmas cards.

We drove past Breakfast Creek, where one of the first explorers had breakfast in the early 1800s, and headed for the nearest pub, where a large notice said 'Shirts are requested to be worn during mealtimes'. Wherever you go in Australia, you are bombarded with sartorial instructions.

Later we passed umbrella trees, the Ithaca Ice Works, the Don Juan Waterbed Shop, and a poodle parlour (where you could have your dog 'fluff dried' for four dollars), but found nowhere open for lunch. It was the Saturday after ANZAC day.

Giving up, we returned to our hotel room, where we were greeted by a fridge full of miniatures, and a ringing telephone. It was two of my husband's ex-warehouse-men, now living in Brisbane, who came over for a drink. When they worked in England, they had always had to struggle to make ends meet. Now, doing the same job, they have their own houses with swimming pools, beautifully cut suits, children at private schools, and enough

14

spare money to take their families out to restaurants whenever they want to. One of them brought his Australian wife. Immediately the sexes divided. My husband talked to his ex-warehousemen, while I talked to the wife, who admitted that any woman who tried to barge in on all-male conversation would be considered a tart.

Brisbane at dusk was magical. The huge river turned to mother-of-pearl under its Meccano bridge, a lemon-yellow sunset gilded the grey-green acacias and softed the rose-pink roofs and the trellis of pylons along the hills. Reeling from jet lag I collapsed into bed and embarked on the first of a series of interrupted nights, this one punctured by Tarzan howls from a wedding party in the next door bedroom.

Sunday Brisbane: Woke feeling profoundly depressed at the thought of trying to promote a book on class in a classless society. Elsa arrived at midday to collect us. She had been staying with her mother, who had told her it was very vulgar to wear white shoes. Driving to lunch, we passed a beautiful hill dotted with large white houses each with its own rich ruff of trees.

'That's the toff area,' explained Elsa. For a moment I thought she'd said 'tough area', but actually the two adjectives are often synonymous in Australia, which boasts a very high population of upper-middle-class criminals – or 'crims' as they are called. Very little stigma is attached to going inside, admittedly not very difficult in Brisbane, where anyone involved in an abortion gets fourteen years, and where it's against the law to go on demonstrations.

We lunched on Filet Tiara with Peter Charlton of the *Brisbane Telegraph* and his wife Helen. Peter, who with his fair hair and reddish moustache looks like an officer in the Scots Guards, was very happy to explode the myth of a classless Australia. Doctors used to be the top of the social scale, he said, but they'd lost caste since the advent of Medibank (Australia's equivalent of our Health Service). Now judges were regarded as the smartest profession (presumably they're also the busiest putting all those 'crims' inside). He finally added that the Australians had hated Brearley because he was too upper class and couldn't bat either.

Touring Brisbane later, we noticed the great number of trees to each house, and the way luscious plants jut out of the most uncompromising yellow rock. We passed the Albert Street Methodist Church, beloved of John Betjeman, with its brilliant terracotta brick, and the fountain which only runs at weekends to save money, of which you can buy plastic replicas for your garden in purple, pink, and blue.

According to Elsa, the river often overflows. Once the first two floors of her office were flooded, and they all rowed in to save the Telex machine. 'When we got there, we all sat round the boardroom table, opened the fridge and drank what was in it.'

On to a rugger match – where a large sign told us that pensioners and schoolboys in uniform would only be charged 22 cents. The ground was pretty soft by Australian standards – at least there was grass on it, but every time anyone took a kick, two minions had to rush on with a bucket and build a sandcastle to hold the ball. The players were so lean and bronzed and fit – it looked more like a beach ball anyway. A man wandered past with 'Save Water' on the front of his T-shirt, and 'Bath with a Friend' on the back. A flock of ibises drifted across the cornflower-blue sky. Gradually it was sinking in that we were really in Australia.

Helen Charlton talked resignedly of the Australian male's obsession with sport. When they were adopting their first baby, Peter rang up his rugger club to explain that he couldn't make training that evening as they had to pick up the baby.

'Why can't you pick it up tomorrow?' asked the captain in deepest indignation.

Helen had also given up making rugger teas. There was

not much joy in making hundreds of sandwiches and cream cakes, if all the players did was hurl them at each other.

At half-time, a siren went, and everyone ate crumbled vealies, Dagwood red sausages and square pies. Australia is a land of harsh rules, which everyone breaks. Another large sign by the bar announced that liquor must not be consumed beyond this point, but was defied by a shingle of empty tins all round the boundary – a sort of Beer Canute.

Peter, a member of the TA, took us back to his officers' mess after the game. Looking at the regimental silver, and the photographs of moustacheoed, double-barrelled DSOs round the walls, one realized how English some of Australia is, and understood, for the first time, the bitterness at our joining the Common Market.

'It is very hard,' said Peter, 'for us whose fathers fought and died in the war to have to queue to get into England, while men from Germany walk straight through.'

We dined with Blair Edmunds, who runs the largest local radio station, and who looked like Hermann Prey. His friend, Ian, is a schoolmaster, with wonderful blackberry dark eyes. They have two Afghans, a beautiful house full of paintings, and a bright green loo seat. Other guests included a high-court judge who'd recently won a Father of the Year award, and his wife, a deliberately understated American academic, who promptly told us that, as a fine arts professor, she earned one of the highest salaries in Australia.

Dinner was wonderful, cooked by Blair and Ian, and consisting of palest green courgette soup, followed by mammoth prawns called Morton Bay Bugs, duck in black cherry sauce, and home-made pistachio ice-cream – all to a background of the eight sides of *Fidelio* played *fortissimo*.

For a classless society, conversation was decidedly up-market. Someone exquisitely described a socially ambitious neighbour as being 'Not only self-made, but self-hyphenated as well'. The judge told me he came from a distinguished family. His wife described the size of her family vault, and the family silver given to her grandfather by the King of Morocco. Recently she'd met Prince Charles when he visited Australia, and regarded him as a considerable intellectual. They had sat together on a sofa, kicked off their shoes to relieve their aching feet, and discussed mezzo-sopranos.

'Charles,' she added emphatically, 'knows his Grace Bunbury *(sic)* backwards.'

Talk moved on to the ostentation of the local millionaire, who on being awarded the OBE had it made up in diamonds as a single ear-ring. He also had the 'J' of his sheep brand made into diamond ear-rings for his wife. Lunching with him recently, guests had been slightly startled when a particularly handsome stallion kept flashing past the window like a windscreen wiper. Later they discovered the horse was being specially whipped back and forth by a couple of farm-hands.

Finally, the judge launched an attack on the appalling meanness of the English – particularly the upper classes. An aristocratic couple and their grown-up son had evidently recently descended on him for a fortnight without asking.

As his wife was away, the poor judge had had to cook for them three times a day. (On one occasion the son was going into town and he asked him to pick up a bottle of milk and was promptly asked for the money.) Finally, after a week, unable to bear it any longer the judge had fled to Sydney, whereupon they demanded housekeeping money for their remaining week.

Having experienced generous and riotous hospitality ourselves we slunk to bed at 1.30, feeling bitterly ashamed of our countrymen.

Monday Brisbane: Picked up at 8.30 for my first radio phone-in. Shakes were not entirely due to nerves. The interviewer had a beard, wore khaki shorts, glared at me

18

fiercely, and gave me a far from easy ride on class distinction in England. Afterwards people rang in, English immigrants grumbling at how undisciplined Australian children were, Australians grumbling at how dictatorial and unimaginative English parents and nannies were. My interviewer looked even more disapproving and, while I was stumblingly answering a question on poverty in England, shoved a note across the table which divided us. On it he had written:

NUN (*to Mother Superior*): We have a case of VD.
MOTHER SUPERIOR (*absent-mindedly*): Oh, put it in the cellar, it will make a nice change from the usual Beaujolais.

With great self-control I managed not to scream with laughter, but my answer on poverty was not as lucid as it should have been.

Radio stations in Australia are amazingly smart, shag-pile on the wall, beautiful girls and forests of plants at every entrance. At the next station, I talked to Hayden, who was polite and elegant and an ex-minister; and at the next, to Alan, who had slanting fox's eyes, said he was hungry, and that I sounded like an upper-class wanker when I called people 'Darling'. I'd get on much better in Australia, he added sternly, if I addressed people as 'Pal' or 'Chum'. Felt this was too reminiscent of dog food ads to carry real conviction in my case. As we left, the weather men who had predicted rain were peering anxiously out of the window at an untroubled sapphire-blue sky.

On to the University of Queensland, surrounded by vast yucca plants, the crevices of which everyone used as litter bins. Interviewed by bad-tempered girl with short hair and a large bottom, who told me truculently that their station accepted no advertising, or government support, and that all staff decided their own salary — and asked what England was going to do about poverty. Talked woollily about National Assistance and Legal Aid, and totally failed to insert the words 'Pal' or 'Chum'.

Leaving the Too Wong Baptist Church, Oscar Wilde Street, and Chippendale Street, we climbed up a winding road through forests of eucalyptus trees to Channel 7. Very disappointed not to see koala bears, but Elsa said they would be asleep in the trees, probably zonked out on eucalyptus leaves.

On reaching Channel 7, we found the entire television station in a state of uproar because they'd been stealing all Channel 9's celebrities and Channel 9 had been stealing all theirs. Elsa whispered that my navel was showing in my cream jump suit, and handed me a safety- pin. Interviewed by very beautiful girl in a beige dress called Donna who said she *had* been going to read my book, but she'd gone camping instead.

Collapsed into nearest bar, and drank two huge Bloody Marys. If every day was going to be as rigorous as this, I'd never stand the pace. Yet another notice warned us that the Management would refuse service to anyone not properly dressed. Perhaps Elsa's safety-pin had been a good idea after all.

The bar overlooked a dusty track lined with palm trees, and white slatted houses backing on to mysterious dark-green mango groves. In the scorching sunlight, the influences seemed to come from New Orleans, the Wild West, and India all at the same time. But round the corner instead of Gary Cooper with a bootlace moustache, came the postman bicycling in shorts. Elsa said that when she was a child, the postman went on his rounds with two horses, one to ride, the other to carry the mail.

On to Channel 9, which was also in an uproar because the man who'd been going to interview me had been stolen that morning by Channel 7, and a new presenter had just taken over. The make-up people had been rather over generous with the Pan-stik, and he now had a bright yellow face like a large Jaffa orange. The telephone rang continually with journalists clamouring for interviews. He had been going to read my book, he said apologetically, but alas someone had stolen it. At least he hadn't gone camping. 'Did I feel Australia was a classless society?' 'No,' I said, 'it's full of upper-middle-class crims.'

SYDNEY
Flew to Sydney feeling utterly knackered. One symbol of the Australian good life is the confetti of bright-blue swimming pools beside every house seen from the plane as you come into land. Everyone in Sydney seemed to be wearing Campari-pink track suits. On the way to our hotel, we passed another Don Juan Waterbed shop, and a man's hairdresser called Stallion, which had a sign outside of a rearing horse with a luscious Carmenrollered mane.

Tuesday Sydney: Spent absolutely punishing day whizzing from radio stations to television studios, being followed by beautiful lynx-eyed journalist called Gail Heathcote, and moustacheoed trendy photographer — a sort of Denim Lillee.

First interview with John Laws, who, I was warned beforehand, 'has quite a good personality' (whoever she might be). He turned out to be lean, craggy and has attractive as a Western Hero, and clad from his Seiko watch to his Gucci boots in status symbols. He is also very rich, having just sold his house for £1,000,000 to the Iraqis, and gave me the first flicker of an eye-meet I'd had since I'd landed in Australia. Felt as euphoric as a teen-ager, but before I had time to score, I was whipped on to next interview. Everyone kept harping on how classless Australia was, a supposition belied by some magazines I flipped through between programmes. One had a long feature on Australia's twelve most eligible men; another ran a long feature in which a girl thanked her mother for scraping and saving to send her to private schools and later paying for elocution lessons to iron out her working-class accent.

Lunched in a marvellous restaurant called You and Me.

21

Australian food is superb if you like solid slabs of protein. Steak, lamb, fish and shellfish are all wonderful, but vegetables tend to be very boring – you usually end up with the inevitable salad, thick layers of lettuce through which the dressing never penetrates. One found evidence of this attitude in the high streets, where incredibly tidy greengrocers' windows look as untouched and protected as jewellers'. As if in protest people walk along the crowded pavements eating fruit salad and cream out of bowls.

After a frantic afternoon I was left with a quarter of an hour to change for a launching party, in an old wine cellar. Arrived miraculously on time to find it packed. Where there's free drink, Australians always manage to be punctual. At parties there is a 'launcher', someone who organizes the party and makes a speech of welcome. Mine, on this occasion, was the ex-daughter-in-law of the ex-Archbishop of Canterbury (who no doubt once danced with the girl who danced with the man who danced with the Prince of Wales). She made an eloquent speech, as did my Australian publisher, who on a recent visit to the Garrick Club in London, was heard to make the immortal remark: 'There's nothing wrong with the place that couldn't be improved by a few fruit machines.'

Spent entire party being interviewed upstairs by various local radio stations. Made fleeting appearance in party room, not unlike Banquo's ghost. Overheard girl asking: 'Is Jilly Cooper actually here in person?'

Left my husband to have a much deserved night off with an old school friend and his wife, and set off with Elsa for the John Singleton Show, which has one of the highest ratings in Australia. Fortunately I had no time to be nervous. John Singleton has straw-coloured hair, and that monochrome-brown complexion, without any tinge of pink or red, rather like peanut butter, that is so common in Australian men. He was dressed like a Union Jack: blue suit, red tie, blue and white striped shirt with a white collar. Despite managing to resemble a coastguard and a basking shark at the same time, he has an excellent sense of humour. Up to the first commercial break, we fooled about enjoying ourselves.

Alas, in the second half of the programme Eartha Kitt was one of the guests. Having worshipped her for years, I was about to ask for her autograph, when she turned on me like an alley kitt, saying the book (which she hadn't even looked at) was junk, that I was junk, and all social distinction was junk. Fortunately, we were divided by the bolster of another guest, a massive wrestler, who cheerfully admitted his accent always got thicker as the evening wore on.

Miss Kitt then screwed up her otherwise pretty face like an old prune and asked John Singleton to pass her 'that book'. John Singleton looked bewildered and picked up my book which was on the table. 'No, not that junk,' snarled Miss Kitt, but the real book under the table, which turned out, despite Mr Singleton's amazement, to be written by himself, and which fell open at a marked place where several lines had been underlined. Miss Kitt then read out some sententious claptrap about the dignity of all men, and all men being equal and brother to one another. She then re-sharpened her claws on me, and asked what I was going to do with all the money I'd made. Replied rather nervously that I was going to pay my debts. Mercifully we were both obliterated by the commercial break.

Thinking things could only get better, Elsa and I went on to a very good party in the smart Sydney suburb of Wallhura. Talked first to handsome man who had made films as a tax loss, and whose name in Polish is evidently as smart as Windsor in England, then to beautiful woman, who was convinced her last lover was murdered: 'We didn't even have a row, he simply disappeared one day.' She was also concerned about her dog, which she part-owned with a barrister down the road. Unfortunately the barrister had just gone inside for a couple of years, so her nanny had to spend hours every day chauffering the dog over to the barrister's girlfriend who lived on the other side of Sydney. This story was capped by a lissom ex-model with kingfisher-blue eyes, who said she was going to publish a diary of everything she ate and excreted during her pregnancy. Her husband, who writes the script for the Paul Hogan Show, had evidently filmed and tape-recorded her during labour.

Slightly bemused, but easily the best-looking couple in the room, were a man of military bearing in his fifties and his wife who looked like Lady Longford. They turned out to be the parents of Sam Neill, the New Zealand born male star of *My Brilliant Career*. We then had an extremely enjoyable conversation discussing Sam's beauty and talent, and Welsh cobs, which they bred in New Zealand. Discovering I was also staying at the Menzies Hotel, they gave me a lift back. Kept saying what a shame it was they hadn't met my husband, as he was a military publisher and I knew how well they would have all got on.

As we drew up at the Menzies Hotel I saw my husband in reception being watched with very jaundiced eyes by the night staff. He and old school friend, and old school friend's wife were all playing pig-in-the-middle with a large pink panti-girdle. In the lift down, my husband had evidently patted the wife on the bottom, and remarked that he detested roll-ons, whereupon she had promptly whipped hers off. They had already mislaid two keys to our bedroom, and were too chicken to ask the hotel staff for a third.

The wife now fortunately had the presence of mind to thrust her panti-girdle behind her back, and my husband and his old school friend more or less composed their features as I introduced them very hurriedly to Sam Neill's parents. In recognition of their team spirit I was the one who had to wheedle a third key out of jaundiced night staff.

In bedroom we found two keys and finished off free champagne, thoughtfully but perhaps unnecessarily provided by management. Bed by four.

Wednesday Sydney: Woken at eight by breezy radio telephone interviewer. Too busy holding my head on with one hand, and the receiver with the other to be very coherent on English social structure. Was even less so when second telephone interviewer rang at 8.20. Elsa collected me at nine to go on the Caroline Jones Radio Show, which she stressed had huge ratings and was crucial to sales of book. On the way there, we passed the shark fin of the Opera House, and the Traditional Boomerang School. Felt mine had returned several times already.

Interviewed by Old Etonian with charming manners called Michael Morton Evans. Pale, anorexic lady, looking like one of Tennessee Williams's sexually strung-up heroines, made an awful fuss about reading the weather beforehand. Thought reprovingly to myself that in England weather people knew their place and quietly moved cloud bricks around screens without bothering anyone else.

Interview went excellently until Michael asked me if I were a snob. Replied that if I am, my children frequently cut me down to size, and that my son was once overheard saying to a little friend in awed tones: 'Mummy says "pardon" is a much worse word than "fuck".' Interview moved briskly on to another theme, and then ended somewhat abruptly.

'Well that was nice,' I said, only then noticing that the weather lady had turned pea green.

'Do you realize,' she said in a trembling voice, 'that by using that dreadful word, you have probably lost me my job?'

Just wondering how anything I'd said could possibly affect the weather, when I realized that the pea-green lady was in fact Caroline Jones, and I had put up a monumental black by using a four-letter word. Michael Morton Evans, though ashen, took it very well, rather like the A. E. Housman soldier, who smiled and kissed his fingers to the enemy as he was being bayoneted. Would

The Sunday Times give him a job, he said, if he were sacked. As I left, the switchboard was jammed with outraged callers. Felt extremely contrite, but also that Australian morality was slightly dislocated. On John Singleton's programme the night before Barry Humphries had made a fleeting appearance, saying Edna Everage was going to England to replace the Queen, and he hoped everyone would give that little lady the Clap.

By early afternoon the four-letter word story had reached the evening papers. I slunk back to the Menzies hoping to catch a couple of hours' sleep before flying to Canberra, to find our bedroom full of more of my husband's ex-warehousemen, and him on the telephone saying: 'Come over at once. Jilly'd adore to see some children, she's missing our own two terribly.'

Both statements at that moment were totally untrue. My husband it turned out was speaking to an ex-nanny of ours who now lived in a church, and who arrived with two charming but extremely boisterous children, who proceeded to wreck the place. One disappeared into the bathroom for several minutes and was discovered cleaning its teeth with the lavatory brush. Felt slightly comforted that ex-nanny had as little control over her children, as she had accused me of having over mine when they were the same age.

Later we descended to the hotel bar to be confronted by a solid phalanx of males drinking as if their wives depended on it. 'In England,' said one of the warehousemen's wives, 'men go home after work and then take their wives out for a drink. Here they go straight to the pub, and their wives never know when to expect them home.'

'Macho' is a word on everyone's lips in Sydney, which after San Fransisco has the highest homosexual population of any city in the world. People attribute this to the cameraderie and essential chauvinism of the Australian male, but also to the fact that Sydney is principally a beach society, where the men take great care toe cultivate beautiful bodies, which frequently leads to narcissism. If you admire yourself in the mirror continually you start fancying similar images. Perhaps someone should write a novel about Sydney called *Crim's Fairy Tales*.

One spin-off of such a chauvinistic society is the ritualistic adulation of Mum. While we were in Australia, the whole nation was revving up for Mothering Sunday, which is held much later than in England. Every hotel offered Mother's Day banquets, dinners or luncheons – presumably to compensate for the deprivation Mum suffers during the rest of the year. Mother's Day present suggestions in advertisements included cars, fur coats, panti-girdles (again) and, even more bizarrely, electric organs.

CANBERRA

Fly to Canberra and dine with very glamorous press attaché at a Malayan restaurant, which, also mercifully perhaps, had mislaid its corkscrew. I commented *sotto voce* on the attractions of the press attaché. 'I thought so too,' said Elsa. 'Until he took me back to his flat for the first time, and I was confronted by his eight children, his wife and his wife's lover.'

Bed at the Ethos Motel by one thirty in the morning. My husband and I had reached that pitch of exhaustion when one smells one's clothes to see if one has worn them, and makes cups of coffee out of the sachets of shoepolish thoughtfully provided by the motel. We also kept waking each other up in the night by mistakenly turning on the air-conditioner, which let out a deafening roar, instead of the light.

Thursday Canberra: By some miracle, my husband (totally unaided by me) got us packed and on parade by 8.30 a.m. He was understandably irritated when I kept referring to him as 'Kerry Packer'. The day's schedule included endless radio and press interviews and a harrowing networked speech to the National Press Club.

Drove through Canberra with its tidy gardens and ring of slate-blue hills. Autumn leaves were tumbling from the plane trees, but rushes marred the perfection of the artificial lakes. Gum trees with their leprosy-white trunks and dank leaves lined the streets like corpses rising from their graves at the time of the Crucifixion. Pale sunlight fingered the dried-up fields. The Australians smothered in jerseys chuntered about the cold. I revelled in the gentler weather.

Two tents were pitched outside Government House. In one, said our taxi driver, lived a man protesting against paying too much alimony; in the other, a life pensioner injured in an accident, who considered his compensation insufficient. In Australia one finds far less subservience than in England. There people stand up for their rights. Journalists, for example, went on strike at the last election because they felt the political coverage was too right-wing biassed, and their air hostesses on Australia's chief internal airline also came out on hearing that one of the bosses had described them (not inaccurately) as a 'lot of old broilers'.

Satire seems to proliferate in countries with powerful governments, apparently buoyant economies and free speech. Just as *T.W. 3* and *Private Eye* blossomed during the never-had-it-so-good era of the sixties, in Australia one sees evidence of this in the endless graffiti and the disrespect shown towards the Government and particularly its rather stolid Prime Minister, Malcolm Fraser, Expressions like 'I've a Fraser of a Day', or 'Things will get Fraser before they get better', have passed into the language.

The night before I spoke to the National Press Club, the much publicized first telephone call between Mrs Thatcher and Malcolm Fraser had been shown on television. Whiling away the time before the call came through, the Canberra Press Corps had offered a prize to the journalist who produced the most likely version of their conversation. The winning entry went as follows:

MRS THATCHER (*picking up telephone*): Hello. (*Sound of very heavy breathing follows.*) Oh not you *again*, Malcolm.

Probably sensing my terror at speaking in public, the Press Club audience were incredibly kind and even laughed quite a lot. Questions afterwards were trickier. Having been asked what class Mrs Thatcher was, I said 'originally lower-middle', and went on to imitate her voice: 'slow and deep to cover up any trace of an accent.' I then suddenly realized that Mrs Thatcher's daughter Carol, who works on an Australian paper, was in the audience and found myself back-pedalling frantically and saying how wonderful Mrs T. was really, on the whole.

MELBOURNE
Immediately afterwards we flew to Melbourne for another launching party. Below us the gum trees were draped over the mountains like moleskin counterpanes. As a fellow passenger pointed out the range where Ned Kelly carved out his legend I experienced a sudden burst of frustrated rage that we were to get no chance to get out of the towns to the real Australian wild.

By way of compensation when we reached the party in Melbourne, the wild had, in some measure, come to us. Our 'launcher', Captain Peter Jansen, owns a huge flat on top of the Windsor Hotel, which appeared to be inhabited by vast tropical plants, wild animals, predatory looking pressmen, and exotic girls. The drawing room to which I was immediately dragged for the inevitable television interview was a taxidermist's heaven.

'Jansen's going through his stuffed period,' explained one of the cameramen. As I reclined on a sofa, covered in kangaroo, zebra and lion skins, watching my black dress rapidly gathering golden fur, a bison in a top hat, and a bear in a flying helmet, and various heads of big game stared glassily down at me. In an alcove was a Norman window made of stone, and an old organ, which Peter Jansen plays in moments of stress.

Jansen himself is something of an enigma. His printed card boasts that he will fight wars, tame tigers, pacify wives, start and quell uprisings, plot assassinations, but it provides no address. He also steeplechases in England, show-jumps, motor-races, owns a fleet of double-decker buses, which he hires out, and owns several cats, a tame dingo, and a chocolate-brown Dobermann who all live on the roof.

In his late thirties, he is exceptionally good-looking with piercing speedwell-blue eyes, a swarthy skin, and a black beard. No one knows what he's Captain of either, unless it's a grounded pirate ship. Among his friends, he numbers David Somerset, Jonathan Aitken, and Mrs Thatcher, whose children lived with him when they first arrived in Australia. During Melbourne Cup week, he usually has fifty people to stay. One year the guests included Harold Macmillan's grandson, who had such a good time that he stayed for a fortnight wearing the same clothes. Finally the rest of the household, unable to bear the bouquet of their English guest any longer, picked him up and threw him, clothes and all, into a full bath.

Later Jansen introduced me to his dingo, who had watchful amber eyes, long blond fur, and straddled his master's neck like the lamb in the Light of the World painting. The dingo – who doesn't wag his tail like a dog but submits to being cuddled by selected strangers – was friendly but detached, not unlike Jansen himself. Sometimes at night, he howls on the roof, causing visiting graziers, up for Parliament and staying in the Windsor Hotel, to wake up with a start and reach for their shotguns.

Even as a child, Jansen was enterprising.

'When I was eight,' he said, 'I had a thriving business castrating cats with my grandfather's cut-throat razor. I used to buy chloroform from the chemist, put the cats' heads in a gumboot, and charge sixpence a time. I'd completed over 600 operations before my grandfather found out that I was using his razor. He threw up for two days.'

In between interviews, I managed to spend a few blissful minutes talking to various guests at the party. One contradictory aspect of the Australian character is that one moment they'll be boasting of the grandness of their English forebears, and the next regaling you with stories of their outback grandfathers, who stubbed cigarettes out on the palms of their hands, and cracked rattlesnakes like whips.

Friday Melbourne: And on with the treadmill. Cheered up by particularly good interview with Derryn Hinch, a dynamo with thatched hair. When he had first come to Melbourne as a raw young country boy, he said, he had to go to the Windsor Hotel for a press reception. As he was going out of the swing doors afterwards he saw a man in a very smart uniform, and thinking it was the done thing, tipped him liberally. He later discovered that the man who pocketed the tip without a word of thanks was an English Brigadier, staying in the hotel.

Apart from ex-nannies and my husband's warehousemen, Australia seemed to be extensively populated by girls who once went to school with me. After every broadcast, the telephone in the radio station would ring, bringing gales of hearty laughter from some ex-lacrosse captain. Melbourne was no exception: 'Do you remember me? I used to be called Juggins,' said an all-too-familiar voice, 'Now I'm a physiotherapist.'

Unable to cope with Juggins in my present state of collapse, I lied that we were just departing for Adelaide, and spent my remaining time in Melbourne ducking to avoid big-boned forty-year-old women in the street.

Four-letter word story had now reached English papers. Caroline James was quoted as saying she expected her guests to exercise decorum. Thought what a nice name Decorum would be for a dog, then you could exercise it every day. I was quoted as saying I couldn't see anything wrong with four-letter words, and everyone used them all the time on the BBC. Suddenly had vision of Kenneth Kendall locking solemnly into the camera, and saying: 'Now we've had the bleeding news from Rhodesia and the American election, let's turn to the fucking weather.'

Made lunchtime speech to National Book Council in ritzy venue called the Stardust Room, which rather incongruously had bright-green walls. One of the audience said he hadn't had such awful food since he was in hospital.

Saturday Melbourne: Blissful morning off. Longed to lie in bed, but felt we ought to look at Melbourne. Classical rather than romantic, the city is twice the size of London with half the population, and gives the impression of space and calm. Pavements are wide, parks everywhere, trams grumble and chunter along the streets. The huge tree-fringed river, with its paddle steamers and wide banks, has plenty of room to breathe as it weaves its stately way past great golden houses. Parliament House opposite our hotel has hundreds of steps up to the front door, allegedly to discourage demos and petitioners. The Australian sense of humour, however, does not go for long without asserting itself. The statue of a seated General Gordon had a beer can in his lap.

We took a brief look at the National Gallery, and admired the Nolans with their lobelia-blue skies and papier mâché rhubarb-coloured hills. There was also a lovely Leonardo drawing of The Virgin and Child with the child trying to hold a struggling cat in his arms. The other paintings tended to be very committed. Instead of worldly cardinals and beauties with pearls and ivory bosoms, you have emigrants weeping on the voyage out, or hacking their first homes out of the bush or workmen sitting in pubs, or working in mines. The most symbolic painting of a perhaps passing Australia was by Arthur Boyd. It showed three shearers engrossed in a candlelit game of cards. One of them, however, had his foot firmly on the train of his bride who was still wearing her white dress, and carrying her bouquet while a red-eyed ram nuzzled knowingly at her stomach. Machismo, chauvinism, possessiveness: it says it all.

In the taxi back to our hotel, the driver told us that any trouble in industry here was caused by Pom shop stewards. He was also the only Australian I heard saying 'Fair Dinkum'.

The rest of the day was spent with Kevin Childs, an extremely funny columnist from *The Melbourne Age* who looks like Woody Allen. He rents a house in a pretty suburb from a PR lady who also owns the next-door house. Because one is not allowed to put out signs advertising the nature of one's business in a residential area, she re-named her houses 'Aspect' and 'Prospect' after her PR company when she moved in. Soon the rest of the street latched on to the idea, and you now have the policeman a few doors down calling his house 'Suspect', a psychiatrist living in 'Introspect', even a parson renaming his vicarage 'Circumspect'.

Belting through eternal suburbs, we passed houses called 'Panache' and 'Charme', and a road sign saying 'Natives: 1 dollar 50'. Then, as the country grew more wild, another sign saying 'Kangaroos Cross Here'. To the right, rising out of the tufted trees, was a red castle. 'Goes all the way back to the early 1970s,' said Kevin Childs.

Since Michael Davey, late of *The Observer*, took over the editorship of *The Melbourne Age*, the standard of writing has improved dramatically. According to Kevin, the journalists are actually learning to write English. One girl reporter, however, still has the reputation for producing purple prose. The other morning she wandered into the office grumbling how ill she felt. 'Perhaps,' said the features editor, 'it was something you wrote.'

33

Australians tend to drop in unannounced far more often than the English, but always bring food and drink if they do. That day we had been invited to lunch with Clifton Pugh, one of Australia's most successful painters, and Kevin's boot clanked with dozens of bottles every time we rounded a corner. Another attractive rural habit is the way people always wave to each other if they pass on the road. If you're negotiating too difficult a bend to take your hands off the wheel, you simply raise a finger.

Clifton Pugh and his companion Judith lived in an extremely glamorous two-storey mud hut in the middle of a gum tree wood. Clifton built the place with his own hands, and, on a long visit, authoress Naomi Mitchison helped him decorate the outside walls with huge painted suns and breasts. On the right of the path up to the door was a rusty piece of farmyard machinery, on the left a pen for the tame wombats.

Clifton Pugh looked like John Bratby's more prosperous rugger-playing younger brother. Judith had soft ash- blond hair, a pink-and-white unmade-up face, wore sea- green Andy Pandy trousers, and exuded a lascivious innocence straight out of Renoir. Despite her child-bride appearance, she holds down a high-powered job, principally teaching women to give birth more easily. She is also heavily involved in the pro-abortion movement. Clifton, who tends to be genial but taciturn, often uses her to distract and relax his sitters by chatting to them while he paints. A case in point was Prince Philip, who, Judith said, was very brusque and uptight during the first sitting, but had become a great friend by the time the portrait was finished.

Clifton showed us a Constable he had picked up for £12 in a London junk shop, and then his last series of paintings which featured a beautiful, acrobatic redhead involved in a sequence of erotic encounters with an emu. 'That model used to be our astrology correspondent,' said Kevin Childs.

Wandering about the house was an utterly enchanting

wombat, which had cream-coloured fur, a square face, a blond suede nose, very small knowing eyes, and furry trousers above long black claws. As solid as a large emery bag, it moved about the house with a slow dignity, suddenly belied by little skips like the mountains in the psalms. When Judith had a miscarriage recently, Clifton smuggled the wombat into hospital every night for a cuddle.

Yet another endearing trait of the Australians, is an almost English silliness about animals. During the time of conscription for the Vietnam War, the Pughs filled in a recruiting form in the name of an earlier wombat called Algernon Hooper Pugh, suggesting he should be a sapper because he was so good at tunnelling. Some weeks later, Hooper received his call-up papers. When he didn't show up, a warrant was put out for his arrest, and when the police kept turning up at the house in an attempt to find him, they were told that Hooper was a student and had probably gone underground. Clifton was even quoted in the local press, as saying 'if Hooper comes back we shall stand by him'.

Some visitors are not as pixillated as we were by either the house, which is regarded as one of the great Australian showpieces, or the wombats. One African General on a state visit was deeply offended when brought there to lunch. He sat sulking on his shooting stick in the drawing room occasionally getting off it to take a swipe at the calves of the female guests and declaiming that, in *his* country, only peasants lived in mud huts and had pigs in the drawing room.

Lunch was delicious but simple: *pâté de campagne*, followed by tagliatelle with green pistou sauce and various salads. We sat on the verandah, which had a twelve-foot drop into the valley below, with grey-gold light filtering down through the ceiling of gum trees. The wombat sat nearby eating mint from a tub to sweeten his breath, while the Pugh's dog, a large borzoi, tried in semi-playfulness to nudge him over the edge. Other livestock included a cockatoo who'd been known to chew up paintings, and whose favourite catchphrase was: 'No, no, Mr Pugh, I'm only an artist's model.'

Conversation ranged from a mean police inspector, known locally as 'Crime Doesn't Pay'; to Melbourne itself, 'half the size of Brompton Cemetery and twice as dead'; and to how deeply they felt about the Vietnam War in which 6,000 Australians had served. Meanwhile, without my realizing it, the local mosquitoes were having an equally delicious lunch on my ankles.

Before leaving, we visited the Pugh's emu, which had a very small head, huge prehensile feet, a large feathered body like a thatched roof, and a wandering beak. Giving me my second eye-meet since I'd arrived in Australia, he pursued me briskly round the field, and then pinned me yearningly against the gate.

'He's certainly fallen for you,' said Clifton, making no attempt to rescue me. 'He's been frightfully frustrated since his fiancée Wilhemenia died.'

Not wanting to emulate Leda, or the redhead astrology correspondent, I made an excuse, and bolted under the barbed wire.

Fleetingly on the drive home we saw the full beauty of the Australian countryside — a grey dusk seemed to smoulder in a valley of silver trees with a rose-pink sky above, and suddenly kangaroos came bounding past, bent double like arthritic old men.

Spent a sleepless night, tormented by mosquito bites and frantically trying to turn off the tropical central heating in our hotel bedroom, which, as we were now entering the Australian autumn, was turned on full blast. My husband put his shoes outside the door with a note saying 'please remove wombat scratches'.

Sunday Melbourne: Lunched out at the beach with bookseller, Philip Jones, and his friend Barry Reid, who is a poet, short-story writer, and chairman of the National Book Council of Australia.

Despite an exquisitely gentle day, with a slight haze over a peacock-blue sea flecked with seagulls, Philip Jones said that everyone was bored with the summer now. Realized for the hundredth time the therapeutic powers of the sea. After half an hour wandering barefoot along the white sand, paddling and watching dogs chase sticks and snap at the heels of passing riders, I felt almost human again.

Philip and Barry's beach house is rented, because a few years ago their own lovely beach house was tragically burnt down, destroying their letters and photographs, Barry's poems and stories, and nearly all their collection of paintings.

During the fire a kindly neighbour had rushed in and systematically started wrapping cheap glasses in tissue paper, and stacked them in boxes. Fortunately another neighbour rushed in crying 'Don't bother with that, save the paintings.' Alas, they were only able to fight their way into the smoke-filled rooms and rescue one of the Nolans. But this was later sold to the Australian National Gallery for enough money to pay for the building of a new beach house.

Barry and Philip used to know Nolan very well. When he was young, said Barry, he was evidently as beautiful as Robert Redford in *The Great Gatsby*. He was also a wonderful athlete and could dive from a great height into manholes.

Other guests at lunch included a handsome woman called Celia who 'used to be published' and who said Australia was a cultural desert; and an author called Maurice, who refused to tell me the plot of his children's story in case I pinched it — fear of upper-middle-class crims again, I suppose. He did however wax eloquent on the subject of his English mother-in-law, who'd come out to stay last summer, and never stopped grumbling about Australia until he'd thrown her out of the house, driven her to the airport and booked her on the next plane home. Next day she'd rung up still in Australia, and apologized, and he'd never had any trouble with her again. Another guest, a glamorous divorcee, said that her Australian mother-in-law was so forceful a character that when one of her chilaren was sent to a remand home for stealing, she'd stood up and told the judge the child couldn't possibly be committed until the following day, as the whole family had tickets that night to see the film of *The Ten Commandments*. Whereupon the judge meekly agreed.

Another perfect, simple lunch: chicken soup and kedgeree, and someone had bought a cake for pudding. Charlie, Philip Jones's genial yellow labrador, rushed round the table pulling off everyone's napkins. A pillar of Melbourne society, Charlie frequently goes out to the newsagent's to buy cigarettes, or takes a thousand dollars in his mouth to the bank.

'We parted company with our bank recently,' said Philip. 'But unfortunately Charlie didn't; he kept dropping in with cheques, and curling up for whole mornings under the old bank manager's feet.'

Back into Melbourne along the coast road, where the suburbs never seem to begin or end. Soft Indian summer colours were provided by the scarlet glow of mountain-ash berries, and the flaming orange of the turning sumac. Out at sea, the rain descended in a great Wedgwood-blue cloud flanked with amethyst and amber on either side. We passed three joggers, a husband in denim shorts, and a mother and little daughter in matching Laura Ashley dresses, hurrying not to get caught in the rain. 'Only the middle classes jog,' said Philip Jones disparagingly. 'The upper classes are thin enough not to need to, and the working classes are too tired.'

Outside our hotel, on the steps of Government House, there was a clash of demos between the pro- and anti-abortion lobbies. Broken placards lay all over the road. Furious frizzy-haired girls – sort of Harpy Marxes – were being driven off yelling in police vans. The two factions (principally composed of barefooted men with their hair tied back, and earnest-looking women in dirndl skirts with big hairy bicycling legs) seemed virtually interchangeable, except the Antis looked more oatmeal and rosycheeked and the Pros more butch and truculent.

'Love and let live,' howled the Antis. 'Save the unborn child.'

'My uterus belongs to me,' yelled back a hefty looking Pro in a canary yellow T-shirt.

'Can't imagine anyone else wanting it,' said a wag in the crowd.

'Anyone who's been arrested, stand on the wall, and we'll organize bail,' shouted a woman in dungarees into a megaphone. Both sides looked thoroughly disconsolate that the confrontation hadn't been more dramatic. Three policemen riding beautiful horses, two greys and a dark bay with long manes and tails, stood on the sidelines being shouted at.

'End police attacks,' chanted both sides, 'on Gays, Women, and Blacks.'

'Not the church not the state, women must decide their fate,' screamed a girl in a leather jacket.

The policemen advanced slightly.

'Up rode the troopers, one, two, three,' murmured my husband. The crowd dispersed.

'Let's all march on the police station,' said a fat woman in a torn cotton dress, dragging a very embarrassed dalmation on the end of a tartan lead. The rest straggled after her, climbing on to their bikes, weaving perilously in and out of the oncoming traffic, until only the loudspeaker man, who'd loaned equipment to both sides, was left behind to load up his van.

On the news later, the demo was played down to a contemptuous three-second flash, and afterwards a fat woman was interviewed because she was about to give birth to her fourteenth 'biby'. 'I always bloom when I'm pregnant,' she said, smiling fatuously into the camera.

Monday Melbourne: And more and more interviews. Feeling that I was about to come apart at the seams, intensified by reading a piece in *The Melbourne Age* filed by the London correspondent before I left, which said I was overweight, had never made it as a writer, used the word 'Darling' too often and lived in an unsmart part of London. Ashamed that I minded his first two observations passionately, and the second two hardly at all. Also livid that I had just rung up his mother in Brisbane, as promised, and told her that her son was doing awfully well in London, and was such a nice boy.

All in all I didn't feel in a very fit state to go on the Don Lane Show that evening. Don Lane is an American who fronts an enormously successful chat show in Australia. More pop than Parkinson, he is less irreverent than Russell Harty, and famous for his professionalism.

A mark of this alleged professionalism was that one of his researchers rang me before I left England, and said they would like me to tell stories about dogs and aristocrats on the programme. Dutifully, I mugged up a string of stories for the pre-interview interview, but was then told Don had changed his mind and would like witty stories on marriages and christenings. Eartha Kitt would also be on the programme, said his research assistant but added, as I backed out of the door, that the organization would be so smooth the two of us would never meet.

Don Lane, who has been voted one of the best-dressed men in Australia, wandered in wearing white jeans and an indigo sweat shirt. With his long face, mournful dark eyes, and mahogany suntan, he looked like El Greco feeling rather guilty about having spent a month on the Costa Brava. Enormously tall, he also has the elegance and apologetic gentleness of a Great Dane. Perhaps as a reaction to a lifetime of people trying to feed him up so he doesn't outgrow his strength, he now lives on bran, grapefruit and vitamin pills.

Having talked briefly about marriages and christenings, he went on to say how rebuffed he'd felt by the

English on a recent visit to London. Many English guests had appeared on his programme before, and had received the full Australian hospitality of dinners out, and long drives into the outback. He'd also moved heaven and earth to help promote whatever plays, records or books they'd come over to push.

Before leaving Australia, they all had given him their numbers in London, begging him to ring when he reached England. However, on arrival, he suddenly discovered every one of these big stars was 'busy'. The only people who looked after him and bothered to return his hospitality were Jackie Collins and her husband. All this might have been understandable if Don were a crashing bore, but he is in fact a man of enormous charm and sensitivity.

The well-balanced Australian has been described as a man with chips on both shoulders. I suspect this chippyness emerges mostly when Australians, accustomed to the generosity, straight-talking and spontaneity of their own countrymen, meet English reserve and superciliousness head on.

Returned to the Windsor Hotel. Attempts to mug up stories on christenings and marriages foiled by arrival of troops of journalists, photographers and, believe it or not, 'Juggins'.

At 8.30 we returned to the studios. Miss Kitt had arrived too and had been secreted away in her dressing room – probably in a cat basket. We crept like burglars past her door and past the glamorous swimming pool built especially for Don outside his dressing room. In the Green Room we were presented with large drinks. A merry band of Irish singers, whose act came after mine, were already stuck into the Bourbon and banging tambourines. One of them managed to knock down a set. Don Lane, now in a nutmeg-brown suit with surprisingly wide trouser bottoms, paid a fleeting visit, rather like the famous surgeon in a very expensive hospital popping in before he removes half your intestines.

Eartha Kitt went on first, and was perfect, growling and purring over Don, and keeping the audience in stitches with her backchat. She was followed by Don and his deadpan side-kick Bert Newton, demonstrating first a balloon bottle-opener, and then clockwork birds, which fluttered round the stage, before crashing to the floor or into the audience, who cackled nervously.

Then it was me. Just as I was about to go on, I saw an old tart approaching me, with a leering blood-red mouth. Recoiled in horror, then realized it was me in a mirror in the full glory of my telly make-up. Too late to bolt, I proceeded down the grey velvet steps, like a guardsman doing the slow march.

'Good luck,' whispered the nice research girl. 'They're a lovely warm audience.' Alas I killed them stone dead, flopping even more dramatically than the clockwork birds. My face became completely rigid as though I were wearing a face-pack. Every funny thought fled my mind. No questions were forthcoming on marriages or christenings, on dogs or even aristocrats. Instead Don started questioning me about the Royal Family, whom I don't know. Felt like the woman who went to one of a certain celebrated French hostess's lunch parties, where the subject for conversation was always decreed beforehand. 'Oh dear,' she said, when asked for her views on adultery, 'I'm afraid I prepared incest by mistake.'

Lamely trotted out a few old chestnuts about Royal Family. The audience looked stony, but not nearly as stony as my husband when I finally came off. He was so incensed by the banality of the interview, that he scrumpled up the free taxi voucher back to our hotel, and stalked out of the studio. As I left the Irish band were singing a rousing ditty called 'When I get Maggie in the Woods'. Bearing in mind current economic gloom in England, felt it would be more pertinent if they'd concentrated on getting Maggie out of the woods. Went to bed with no dinner, which I thought sourly would please the London correspondent of *The Melbourne Age*.

Tuesday Melbourne: Woke in bleakest gloom to find newspapers enraged at my anti-royalist sentiments and my plunging neckline. Vowed to stick to four-letter words in future. From an interview to a death in the morning.

ADELAIDE

Flew to Adelaide. Also ringed by blue hills. Evidently one of the few cities in Australia to be properly designed (the others grew up haphazardly round cattle tracks) it reminded me of Bath, set in the Deep South. The houses in soft ochres and dove greys, with their white balconies and mass of tossing Virginia creeper, seemed only to lack plantations. From every tree came the mewing and complaining of swarms of coloured parrots. The pace was more leisurely here than Melbourne and it was raining, which was rather a relief.

Went on television programme called *A Touch of Elegance*, which had incredibly gracious set, including tufted carpets, a grand piano, and Green-Park-railings paintings. Massed yellow chrysanthemums and gladioli blended in with the amber sofa and armchairs and the glasses of orange juice thoughfully provided for the guests rather than the usual glasses of water. As I arrived, the presenter, Margaret Glazebrook, a charming woman with upswept amber hair, was discussing Mother's Day presents with a lady in a polka-dot shirtwaister with gold seams to her stockings.

'Here's a little sweetie,' cooed Gold Seams, waving a diamanté spectacles case. 'And of course it's *big* fashion news because it's lined with grey velvet, just the right individual gift for someone thinking of Mother – and *who* isn't at this *very* special time?'

She was followed by a man with brushed-forward hair talking about Granny Bonds, and then it was me, followed by hints on potted plants, followed by a languorous young man in a pale-blue suit, playing Chopin on the grand piano with lots of swaying and expansive

43

hand gestures. Barry Humphries is understandably banned from this programme.

Our next interview was at Adelaide University where a poster invited us to a Marijuana Let It Grow Dance with music provided by Mickey Finn and the Teenage Hell Cats.

Very nice launching party at the Standard Book Shop in the evening. Particularly enjoyed myself because there were no interviews, because I met the legendary bookseller and journalist, Max Harris, and because my launcher, this time, was one of my gods, Geoffrey Dutton, novelist, poet and man of letters. Tall, fair, and distinguished he would make the ideal Ashley in *Gone With the Wind*.

At dinner later we talked about the impossibility of being pompous for long in Australia. Geoffrey cited the occasion he had taken a famous opera singer up country and stopped at a village pub for lunch. Afterwards the famous singer, oozing charm and patronage, congratulated the waitress on the excellent coffee.

'Was it Brazilian or Kenyan?' she asked.

'Jeez mate, I don't know,' came the reply. 'It comes out of a 44-gallon drum.'

Bed by 2.30.

Wednesday Adelaide: Up at 8 o'clock. Staggered like a sleep-walker through another round of interviews. Rather appalled to find ourselves diving into the nearest bar to drink large Bloody Marys at 9.30 in the morning. Comforted myself that it was probably six in the evening in England. Despite a cut-out on the door of the Gents' loo of a man in a top hat and tails, a large notice warned us that 'Casual dress only must be worn in this bar'. 'If you came in a dinner jacket,' explained Elsa, 'you might get rubbished.' (Australian for 'mobbed up'.)

She then changed the subject, saying that, according to Australians, 'Poms don't tub.' (Australian for 'English people don't wash'.) You'd go on the underground in London, she said, and everyone's armpits smelled like cottage pie. Leo replied somewhat nettled that this was due to damp newsprint, not sweating armpits, and that we both bathed at least once if not twice a day.

'Baths don't count,' said Elsa disapprovingly. 'How can you possibly bathe in your own slime? If ever I'm forced to have a bath, I have a cold shower immediately afterwards to wash it all away.'

Leo ordered another round. Sensing slight *froideur*, the ever-tactful Elsa changed the subject, saying the Aborigines were a wonderful people ruined by drink.

Felt the Abos were not the only ones – tiddly Pom.

PERTH

We were met by black swans swimming in the airport pond, and two large women holding a banner saying 'Swimming Pool Industry Convention'. We stayed in the New Esplanade Motel, which overlooked the Alf (never Alfred here) Curlewis Gardens. Beyond lay the Swan River which curls through the city, widening and narrowing dramatically, like a vast boa constrictor with various livestock lodged along its body.

Perth – home of Dennis Lillee, Rodney Marsh, Hookes and the Chappell Brothers – has the largest boat-owning population in Australia. It was also the first place that looked exactly as I imagined Australia would do. The sky, that dazzling untroubled blue of Mary's robes in old paintings, arched over endless stretches of perfect lawn dotted with bronzed joggers. Huge white skyscrapers rose out of the river with its fringe of palm trees, and, to the right on a network of motorways, cars whizzed continually back and forth like a child's mechanical toy.

We lunched with Terry Willesey, youngest of the famous seven-strong Willesey family, who are all in television except for one who became a nun. Terry was the best interviewer I encountered in Australia – his choirboy looks and gentle charm belied a steely professionalism.

On the way to the television studios, we passed an old

people's home with a dozen Ferraris parked outside, and a building entirely composed of lavatory tiles called the Hyde Park Hotel.

According to Terry, the upper-middle-class crims were at it again. A big government embezzlement case was due to come up in the supreme court, but, a few days before, party headquarters had been raided and all the documents stolen. An awful lot of Watergates seem to flow under the bridge here. The difference between America and Australia, as Lord George Brown pointed out after a recent visit, is that in America you have to be enormously rich before you attempt to run the country or even a state, whereas in Australia comparatively poor men are voted in and then become enormously rich during office by flogging titles and having inside information on the right property to buy and sell.

In the evening, we went to the theatre to see Trevor Bannister, of *Are You Being Served?* fame, who was playing to packed houses every night in *Rattle of a Simple Man*. Despite a temperature in the eighties, many of the women in the audience turned up in long fur coats. 'Just to show they've got them,' said Elsa. No one took any notice of the warning bells, and as a result both acts started at least a quarter of an hour late – so different from Australian punctuality at parties. Inside the foyer was a door marked 'Crying Room,' to which children are forcibly removed if they start disturbing the performance. Perhaps Caroline Jones should install one.

Friday Perth: Eight-thirty start to face frantic last day of interviews. Went on Lionel York's Radio Show where everyone was fantastically finger-snapping and adrenalized and singing along with the records, and where I nearly sat on a piece of plastic dog muck which had been jokily placed on my chair. Yorkie and his minions screamed with laughter. I giggled weakly, trying to be a sport and not faint with horror.

Yorkie who is Viking blond with the inevitable peanut-butter suntan, wore a plunging black shirt filled with medallions and said he'd been in television and radio for twenty-five years.

How did he look so young? I asked enviously. 'I cherish my body,' he cried joyfully. 'I play tennis, swim, run every morning, and take masses and masses of vitamins.'

He is a very popular figure in Perth.

'We think he jogs upon the water,' said one of his researchers.

Evening — and we bade a tearful farewell to Elsa, who was returning to Melbourne after masterminding our tour with such thoughtfulness and efficiency. Sadness at her departure, however, was tempered by mild euphoria that the last interview was over. Euphoria evaporated ten minutes later with a knock on the door, heralding yet another cameramen from a local paper. 'We're like ants,' he said grinning unrepentantly. 'Kill one, and ten more come to the funeral.'

Saturday Perth: Spent morning buying presents, which included the inevitable boomerang, a fur duckbilled platy-pus with a patent-leather beak, and a wind-up koala bear who plays 'Waltzing Matilda'.

Later we went to an Australian Rules football match known as 'footy', joining Trevor Bannister, who looked very un-Grace Brothers in an immaculate white suit, and his co-star, Rowena Williams, a slinky ash-blond, well known in Australia for her part in the police series *Cop Shop*.

'I play a policeman's wife,' she said, 'and have never moved out of the living room.'

We drove out to the suburb of Fremantle past rows and rows of smart bungalows, all with boats in the second garage and carriage lamps outside the front door. No household is allowed more than two dogs, and if your dog is caught sunning himself on the front lawn, he can be arrested. A blond jogger passed with a poodle on a lead, obviously taking no chances.

We had drinks first with a director of the Footy Club, who lived in an amazingly opulent house with scarlet velvet chairs in the drawing room, Chopin on the piano, *Reader's Digest* condensed books in the shelves and a condensed reproduction of The Night Watch about the electric log fire. Outside purple and pink bougainvillaea cascaded into a kidney-shaped swimming pool. A pretty teenager wandered in to collect a wastepaper basket. Was she the director's daughter? I asked. 'No,' she replied with dignity, 'I am the housekeeper.' (Australian for *au pair*.)

To watch the match, the director's wife wore a mauve velvet dress with a lurex belt and very high heels – so much jollier than the jeans and Guernsey sweater uniform of rugger camp-followers in England.

In the Fremantle headquarters, entitled the W. J. (Nipper) Truscott Pavilion, we had the most wonderful rugger lunch I've ever eaten. Instead of the usual English ham and limp lettuce swimming in Heinz salad cream, we were offered *boeuf bourgignon*, sweet-and-sour fish, crayfish salad, and chicken in almonds, followed by the most luscious selection of puddings, and buckets to drink. Eager women with Vice-Patron badges on their lapels kept sidling up to Trevor Bannister and saying 'You look much younger than you do on television'.

My husband was then taken down to the changing room to listen to the hype before the game, and said he'd never seen players whipped up into such a frenzy of hatred. Australian Rules is big business here, and Fremantle, league winners last year, had lost their first tour matches and were desperate for victory.

The pitch itself was a vast green oval, twice the size of a football field. Above the scoreboard, a large advertisement announced somewhat bizarrely: 'HOWARD CHRYSLER: UNMENTIONABLE DEALS.'

Out came the players on to the field. I've never seen men so fit; their feet hardly touched the ground as they capered about before kick-off. With a game that lasts for nearly three hours and has three intervals you'd have thought they'd want to preserve their energy. Footy rules seem much the same as rugger, except that there are four goalposts each end, and you have to bounce the ball every fifteen yards, pass if you're tackled, and in passing you must punch the ball not throw it. To stop any bias, the Ref turns away from the game and throws the ball in backwards. However this didn't stop a punch-up breaking out between the players before the match had even started.

'Going to be a rough game,' said a female Vice-Patron appreciatively.

There were in fact a surprising number of women in the crowd, principally crones with multi-dyed, wirewool hair, eating huge treble-decker sandwiches and spitting out the crumbs as they yelled their heads off.

'They should have crucified you last week,' screamed one crone, as a member of the opposition was ticked off for dirty play.

'The day someone fills him in, I'll give them a gold medal,' howled her friend.

'Rubbish,' screeched the first, as a Fremantle player missed an easy catch. 'You're as useless as tits on a bull.'

Stars of the Fremantle team were little Budgie, who had black curls, and was desperately quick on his feet like the Maltese Cat, and Peakie, the bearded Captain, who looked like Neptune without his trident, and who is reputed to earn 4,000 dollars (£2,000) a match.

Every few minutes bionic gods, dressed all in sulphur yellow, lope on to the field to give messages to various players. The game often gets so contentious that the refs have to be fast runners too, and come on and off with police escorts. With the four goalposts at each end it is also very easy to notch up huge scores. For the first three quarters it was a very even and exciting game, but gradually and sadly the gallant Fremantle players lost their grip, and in the last quarter, despite the hysterical indignation of their supporters, let the game slip away, losing 143–112. Next I had the dubious pleasure of being the first woman allowed into the Fremantle changing room. Dubious because they were all collapsed on the floor, like a Henry Moore air-raid shelter painting too exhausted and despondent even to roll the Mum Rollette under their armpits.

Afterwards we fought our way into the packed bar to be asphyxiated by a smell of aftershave, quite different from an English rugger crowd – perhaps Elsa had been right about Poms not tubbing. Soon the players shuffled in, pink from the shower and looking somewhat sheepish. Yorkie, a staunch supporter of the club, bounded on to the platform like a mountain goat, and told us not to knock the lads because they were on a temporary losing streak. Everyone cheered, and the day's best players came up to receive their rewards which are usually cash or electrical goods. Evidently Peakie had been awarded television sets so often for being Man of the Match, that he's started his own television-hire firm.

By the time we left, night had fallen. Above us blazed the wonky Southern Cross and there was Orion stretched out drunkenly on his back above the W.J. (Nipper) Truscott sign – as zonked as any of the players.

Returned to our motel to find an Australian friend had turned up with a bunch of gorgeous roses, wrapped in a shocking-pink satin bow, complete with their own vase. Her mother, whom we'd never met, had sent them. She knew we were leaving early next morning, but with typical Australian bounteousness wanted to make our last night a happy one.

Sunday Perth: As we drove out to the airport, we overtook a little trailer. Unlike English trailers, it had no roof, and the horse inside was able to look out over the top. In superb condition, his glossy brown coat gleaming in the sunshine, long mane lifting, he gazed round with bright inquisitive eyes, nostrils twitching as he breathed in the in the fresh morning air. Confident, friendly, generous, ludicrously fit, he seemed to sum up the people we were leaving with such regret. Horsetrailia.

Feminist fatale

Margaret Fink is an Australian feminist, and Germaine Greer's best friend. She also produced, with an almost entirely female team, the film *My Brilliant Career*. Equally successful in Australia Europe and America, the film has already won six awards and had the Queen and Jimmy Carter asking for private views.

Not normally drawn to feminists, it was with trepidation that I arranged to visit Mrs Fink when I was recently in Sydney. Not only, stressed a minion, was she extremely busy, but also extremely upset because her father had just died. The conditions of the interview were that I only stayed a few minutes, and didn't mention her father.

As the taxi drew up at a vast Charles Addams pile festooned with creeper, I was convinced I'd come to the wrong house. You could hear pounding music and roars of mirth all down the street. Inside a riproaring party was under way. Amazingly beautiful people, mostly media luminaries of a slightly indeterminate sexuality, sat round a large table. At the head like a great earth mother exuding glamour and hospitality stood Margaret Fink. She was cutting up a cake to celebrate the birthday of her boyfriend's ex-boyfriend, and trying to persuade an actor called John to marry his girlfriend.

'I will organize the wedding,' cried Mrs Fink imperiously. 'I will even be a bridesmaid.'

John shot an old-fashioned look at his girlfriend. 'At my wedding,' he said, 'you can both be bridesmaids.'

Everyone howled with laughter including the girlfriend, who turned out to be Kate Fitzpatrick, an actress so talented Patrick White writes plays for her.

Next door someone was playing Chopin drunkenly but

very well, while a large strawberry-roan dog called Fido barked in time to the music. Margaret Fink's current boyfriend, a comely scriptwriter called Bill Harding, gave me his American Express card badge to wear to make me feel at home. Margaret reached out to push his black curls back from an exquisitely high white forehead.

'Isn't he beautiful?' she murmured, gazing into his lustrous brown eyes. 'A cross, I always think, between Elizabeth Taylor and Montgomery Clift.'

Had she got time, I asked, for a few questions?

'Come back tomorrow morning,' she said, 'when we're both feeling a lot worse.'

Next morning, we fortified ourselves with pints and pints of black coffee provided by the ever-solicitous Bill.

'He always had boyfriends before he took up with me,' said Margaret proudly. 'We were platonic friends for three years.'

How had they finally got together? I asked.

'We had a fuck,' said Mrs Fink, and roared with laughter.

In a city that after San Francisco boasts the highest homosexual population in the world, attractive heterosexual men are at a premium. Margaret Fink seems to have done an excellent conversion job.

She is one of those rewarding women who can look almost plain, then knock you sideways when she pulls out the stops. That day, her skin – surprisingly fair skin for an Australian – was deathly pale. The slanting eyes – the speckled yellowy-green of a William pear – were heavily shadowed. She has slender wrists and ankles, a voluptuous figure and a self-confessed weight problem in that she wistfully remembers the times when she was very thin.

'In 1971, for example, I lived on vegetable juice for a month, lost a stone, and found a marvellous lover. Unfortunately, I do everything in excess – when I fell in love with an English journalist a few years ago, I had all his suits copied to wear myself.'

53

Born in 1934, the daughter of an insurance inspector, she was exceptionally bright at school. Both parents were shattered when she left home at eighteen to live with Harry Hootin, a distinguished philosopher and drop-out, twenty-five years her senior, who looked like Yves Montand, and who preached a doctrine of hedonism. During ten happy and bohemian years together, Margaret digested much of his philosophy. It was while Harry Hootin was dying of cancer that she met and started an affaire with a millionaire called Leon Fink.

Harry died, and in 1961 she and Leon decided to get married. Naturally she told her friend Germaine Greer, who said in amazement 'My God, Leon Fink was the man who deflowered me.' She had evidently chosen him because he was 'the most upsettingly beautiful man' she'd ever met.

Margaret regarded the early years of her marriage as a time of input. She brought up three children – the eldest is now seventeen – ran her ravishingly pretty house, painted sporadically, and became a very successful hostess.

The marriage was by any standards an open one. Margaret remembers flying in from Europe reeling from jet lag to be met by a distraught nanny wanting a private word. 'Can't it wait till tomorrow?' asked Margeret. The nanny said it couldn't and went on: 'I have to tell you, Mrs Fink, that while you were away I went to bed with Mr Fink.'

'Is that all,' said Margaret with relief. 'For a dreadful moment I thought you were going to give in your notice.'

The turning point in her life was when a friend gave her a novel by an Australian woman writer, Miles Franklin's *My Brilliant Career*. It is very much a modern fairy tale, although written in 1910, of an ugly duckling who turns into a swan, but finally and regretfully rejects the most charming of princes, because she feels marriage and children would stifle her career as a writer.

'It made a deep impression on me,' said Margaret. 'For a long time, I'd felt trapped by domesticity, suddenly I

54

realized that marriage was a lace prison, that for centuries women had squandered their talents, that unless one has money to pay for servants, having a husband and children precludes an artistic achievement. I was determined to make the book into a film.'

A further turning point was reached by 1976, when Leon Fink walked out on her: 'I was absolutely shattered at the time. Now I feel like writing him a thank-you letter. His going triggered me into getting the film off the ground, instead of just talking about it.'

I asked why she had chosen an all-female team.

'I just felt they were all particularly talented. Luciana Arrighi, for example, the production designer, had already designed films like *Women in Love*. I also feel that women who get a chance to work in a male-dominated industry like filming try that little bit harder.'

Even so the road to success was beset with problems. Raising the money was difficult, because backers don't think women have any business sense. At the Cannes Film Festival Margaret and her director Gill Armstrong were treated like naughty schoolgirls. It was only when *My Brilliant Career* was given an almost unheard-of standing ovation that everyone started fawning all over them.

'Other women were jealous of one's success too. It was always women writers who gave the film the more bitchy reviews. Women friends weren't much better, not successful ones like Germaine, but the others who can accept it when you're merely a rich dilettante, but can't bear it if you make the big time.'

As far as feminism is concerned, Margaret believes women should set an example by doing their own thing superlatively well, rather than getting together with a lot of harpies and bellyaching about their lot. She won't go to Women's Lib meetings or demos.

'I hate the word "sexist",' she went on. 'Being anti-men doesn't change anything. The rabid feminists are so anti-glamour, anti-make-up and anti-joy.'

One of the reasons that *My Brilliant Career* was visually

such an astoundingly beautiful film was because Margaret began her working career as a painter, teaching art, and selling every painting whenever she had an exhibition. Then she saw Jean Renoir's film *The River*, and decided colour and form could be expressed more effectively by making films.

Many of the props used in *My Brilliant Career*, including the shoal of silver miniatures on the piano, were Margaret's own pieces. In the dining room, the big table, instead of groaning with food and wine, was now covered entirely by piles of bills. For sadly, despite her ritzy lifestyle, Margaret Fink is flat broke. Although *My Brilliant Career* made a fortune on paper, so far the Australian distributors of the film have only given her £2,500 up front.

'There was an awful row recently,' said Margaret, not without pleasure, 'because I slated them on television.'

'In films,' she went on, 'it's a Catch-22 situation. You must appear rich to get people to put up the money. Anyway I refuse to give up staying at Claridges, and drinking French rather than Australian champagne, and having fresh flowers in the house all the time.' The day before she had bought a sequinned dress for £300, reminding one of Proust's acquaintance, the Comte de Montesquiou, who once complained: 'It's bad enough not having any money, it would be too much if one had to deprive oneself of anything.'

She poured more coffee, and talked of the two formerly unknown stars of *My Brilliant Career*:

'Sam Neill, who plays the rejected Prince Charming, is wonderful to work with — so quiet and easy. He's tipped as the successor to Robert Redford. He's already done two films since *My Brilliant Career*.

'Judy Davis who plays Sybilla wasn't our first choice. We'd already cast another girl, but she had no light on inside her. Judy is marvellous looking, and exudes passion, but she has this absurd belief that she's ugly, clapping her hand over her mouth in a way ugly people often do, which fitted in very well with the character. Like a lot of supertalented people, she was a pain during filming, very uptight, going to bed every night at 8 o'clock, the crew all said she ought to get laid. She was a menace over publicity too. She kept giving interviews saying it was a silly, shallow film, and she didn't like the book. After I told her off, she came to her senses, particularly after she had such a success.'

Would Margaret use her again?

'Of course, talent's much too rare these days.'

As with Byron, you feel that all Margaret's malice is in her pen and her lips, for there is none in her heart.

For a second, gloom seemed to envelop her. 'You know my Dad croaked,' she said. Then, unable to resist a joke: 'The parson who'd never met Dad and Mum went on and on in his funeral address about their 50 years of married bliss. None of us could keep a straight face.'

Life could be worse too. Her bank manager is proud enough of her to give her a decent overdraft, and the other day, she was invited to dine at Government House.

'Butlers and footmen and all that junk,' she admitted with reluctant pride. 'We even separated for the port. I wore a short gold dress by Sonia Rekyll, everyone else was in long dresses. The men were all achievers who were asked to bring their unachieving wives, but no one asked me to bring an unachieving lover. Just think of the taxpayers' money filling all those unachieving bellies just because they're married to achievers.'

A biography of Margaret Fink is already in train. 'Written by a fan, thank God.' I hope it captures her brio and warmth. For the future, she'd like to make a film with Fay Weldon, whom she much admires. At present she and Bill are working on a script together.

'It's a melodromedy, a cross between a melodrama and a comedy, set in the present, about fifteen absolutely frightful people.'

At that moment, handsome Bill came in and gently reminded her it was nearly time to go off and assess films for the Australian Film Commission, and did she want a sandwich.

'A sandwich,' murmured the feminist fatale, putting her arms round him, 'is the last thing I want. If I didn't spend so much time pulling Bill into bed, he might be able to get on with the script.'

Other scenes

Vets' conference

For some sinister reason, three huge copies of *The Hite Report: a Study of Male Sexuality* landed heavily on my desk this week. They make alarming reading. Not only it appears do most American men want sex all the time, but even worse are quite incapable of being faithful to their wives. Partly to avoid the arrival of further copies and to restore my faith in the male sex, I fled to the West Country where the British Veterinary Association were holding their annual conference. I imagined quaffing scrumpy in Common Rooms with rosy-cheeked James Herriots.

Scanning the conference programme on the journey down, I found I had already missed lectures on the uterus of the ewe and ovulation in cows, but could look forward to a talk on sexual aids for cattle which included tail paint for cows, and leg grease and ball markers for bulls. Perhaps I should have stuck with *The Hite Report*.

The Exeter campus swarmed with amiable, healthy-looking men in fawn suits. At a press lunch of cold beef and quiche, the Association President gave us a pep-talk on the low standards of English hygiene.

'Go to an abattoir,' he urged. 'Examine the animals, breathe in the smell.'

'Can one detect salmonella on a carcass?' asked a male journalist earnestly.

Feeling my cold beef churning in my stomach, I fled to the lecture halls but was hijacked on the way by a convoy of delegates driving off to a ram vasectomy demo on the far side of Tiverton.

'I wanted to learn about sexual aids for bulls,' I wailed.

'Our firm makes aids for sheep,' said a balding veterinary supplier from the front seat. 'We market a crayon which straps on to the ram's chest and marks every ewe he's mounted.'

What a splendid check for all those erring *Hite Report* husbands.

Vets certainly drive fast. Herriots of fire, we scorched through the countryside, past lazy ox-bow rivers, magenta fields and beech-wooded hills turning amber in the afternoon sun. As the conversation moved on to dental scaling for dogs, a yellow labrador in a cottage garden grinned at us, trying perhaps to look healthy.

At the demo farm, a crowd of red-faced vets with rolled-up sleeves and thigh-length green gumboots were hanging round a row of sheep-pens. To the right, one group were trying out a rectal probe on pregnant ewes, which huddled together with the dismayed expression of mothers in a maternity clinic invaded by medical students.

The deafening grunts and gushings that issued forth as we tried to distinguish the foetal heart-beat from various more dubious sheep noises were not unlike the sound effects at the start of *Desert Island Discs*. 'They've even issued a long-playing record,' said a vet enthusiastically.

To the left a donnish-looking man in a petrol-blue rubber jumpsuit was showing another group how to collect semen by doing unmentionable things to a poor black-faced ram, who was rolling his eyes like Laurence Olivier playing Othello. Nearby a sandy-haired vet was examining the long yellow teeth of a teenage ewe.

'How does one assess libido in a ram?' he asked thickly.

'Rams can mate up to forty times a day,' answered the donnish man, brandishing a jar of lubricating fluid. 'Now, who hasn't had a go with the ejaculator?'

Shattered I collapsed into the farmhouse, where the rest of the seminar, who'd been performing vasectomies, were wandering round in their stockinged feet, reeking of disinfectant, tucking into vast cream teas.

In a nearby outhouse, a row of rams, who'd already been shaved and given their pre-med, were sitting on bales of hay with their legs apart like elderly aunts at parties.

'Vasectomies don't hurt,' insisted the supervisor, waving a scalpel.

'Ba-a-a-a-lls,' contradicted a dark-brown ram mournfully.

Unable to face any more horrors, I fled back to my little student's room at the University to change for the conference dance. It turned out to be a very jolly affair with a superb dinner, followed by dancing to the music of Ginger Walker – who sounded like a tom cat.

Vets, like sailors, are a fund of good stories. One, who'd just returned from Saudi Arabia, described performing the first emergency Caesarian operation on a camel in the desert.

'Suddenly all the Muslim helpers dropped everything and prostrated themselves in prayer, so all the camel's intestines spilled out on to the sand. All I could do was pray like mad to my own God, and shovel them back again.'

And how they love their animals. Another delegate from Bristol talked about a marvellous guide dog, who gradually appeared to be ferrying her mistress round the city with less and less efficiency. Only on examination, was it discovered that the dog must have been blind for some months.

The atmosphere and Ginger Walker were hotting up.

'Vets drink twice as much as the medical profession,' confided a passing waiter, 'and are four times as nice.'

Certainly there was a friendliness, compassion and enthusiasm about the delegates that one seldom finds in doctors. But then they haven't been soured by thirty years under the Health Service.

Later an attractive man who owned a deerhound called Agatha, and who'd written a paper on mumps in the dog, spent much of the evening telling me in detail how to operate on an egg-bound goldfish.

Next morning, I was able to appreciate the lush beauties

of the Exeter campus with its tropical plants and cascades of gleaming crimson Virginia creeper. On every stretch of perfect lawn were notices complaining 'Your feet are killing me', which were only ignored by the fat squirrels undressing conkers with the dexterity of a Harold Robbins' seducer.

Whipping round the trade exhibition, I was amazed to see how scientific the profession has become. Everywhere vets were playing on computers, or space-invader machines to detect sheep scab. In a few years, they'll evidently be shearing sheep by robot.

Nice to know too that animals have their own etiquette book. On one stand, a tome even longer than *The Hite Report*, entitled *Biology of the Tape Worm*, had a whole section devoted to 'nude rats as hosts'.

Searching for a seminar on pigs, I strayed into a room full of pretty ladies wearing rather too much make-up to tone down après-dance complexions. No, they weren't the pig seminar, they cried with merry laughter, but the Vets' Wives' Benevolent Society, and directed me down the passage to where a handsome delegate in a dung-coloured suit was commendably stressing the importance of public relations.

'Remember the name of your pig farmer's dog – and of his wife too,' he added hastily. 'Listen to his domestic problems as you go round the farm together. If you must criticize his methods, find something to praise as well. It all wins his confidence.'

Inevitably the seminar moved on to sex. Unlike the ram, we were told, boars should only be mated four times a week.

'Did you know,' whispered my neighbour in awe, 'boars take fifteen minutes to ejaculate,' which must be very boaring for the sows. Perhaps one should write a pig best-seller called *Sty With Me Till Morning*.

Pre-lunch drinks with a sweet vet called Archie, who'd written a monograph on venereal diseases in the cow. We were joined by his friend from the Foreign Office, who said male farm animals were often overwhelmed by their responsibilities. He cited one stud bull who'd been flown at great expense by the Milk Marketing Board to service all the cows on a remote Scottish Isle. Let loose, the bull took one look at the eagerly awaiting cows, and walking very slowly up the hill, hurled himself to his death over a cliff.

On to Pedigree Petfoods' Hospitality Room, where we lunched not on Chum or Whiskas-and-soda, but on excellent mackerel and hock. Conversation veered from homosexuality in drakes, to poor snakes who get ulcers from working with strippers.

The day began to take on a lunatic quality. In one hall, a romantic-looking young man in a dark suit was telling a rapt audience about reproduction in the goat. Having covered the role of the udder and the perils of leaving teenage goats unchaperoned, he described an experiment where oestrus had been measured in fourteen goats at Liverpool University.

'We were surprised,' he went on dramatically, 'to find later that all the goats were cycling.' One had visions of them pedalling round the campus in college scarves.

My stomach was getting stronger too, as I was later able to sit without blenching through a riveting lecture on diarrhoea in the dog – complete with slides. Next we learnt about anorexia in the leopard gecko and abscesses in dragons. Finally there was even a *Mite Report*, which had the whole lecture room surreptitiously scratching their heads.

Time for the congress dinner.

'I had to change in such a rush,' gasped a pretty latecomer, 'that my husband offered to sew a button on his evening shirt. He said it was easy – just like stitching up a dog's ear.'

At dinner, I sat next to a gorgeous, ruggedly blond vet from Macclesfield. Having endeared himself by telling me how much he doted on a white bull-terrier, which he'd principally bought to have something around that looked worse than he did in the morning, he then spoilt it all by saying he worked for a drugs firm who bred their own beagles for laboratory tests.

Throughout the conference, I'd made a pest of myself, heckling every vet I met about the horrors of vivisection and factory farming. 'What about battery hens,' I stormed, 'and pigs living on concrete in eternal darkness? What about operations without anaesthetics?' His answer was the same, and as patiently expressed as that of all the other vets. Although he deplored such practices, until the Government make them illegal, or bring in much stricter legislation, all the vet can do is ensure the animals and birds involved suffer as little as possible.

'Anyway,' he countered, seeing I was still looking bootfaced, 'what about the anti-vivisectionists who set fire to a drugs company van, not realizing it was full of rats who all burnt to death?'

Eventually, we made it up, and ended up drinking brandy until two o'clock in the morning with the vet who'd lectured on diarrhoea. As I rather clumsily let myself into my college, I was dimly aware of groaning coming from the depths of a nearby hydrangea bush – ill vet by moonlight.

It was nice to find the profession were as human as James Herriot portrays them. Even so, next morning, I didn't feel up to a lecture on lactating goats or the scrotal hernia of Saul the gorilla, and was very glad my dear husband was coming to drive me home. But there was no escape. Having spent the weekend on a farm in Devon, he lectured me half the way home on the havoc that can be caused to cattle by the warble fly.

The jut set

Nothing illustrates my basic insecurity more than the flap I got into this week before my first trip to Ascot. I wasn't even going in the Royal Enclosure, but my sartorial advisers insisted I must get out of trousers and boots and into a dress, hat and shoes. This meant – horrors – that my legs would have to come out of the closet for the first time in years.

To say that I have table legs would be grossly unfair to a lot of tables. They look passable first thing in the morning, and not bad if I wear lowish heels all day. But half an hour in a heatwave, high heels and tights, and they swell up like duffle bags.

After a baking weekend, I gloomily selected my tropical kit: a straw hat with a blue ribbon, a peacock-blue dress, with my legs coming only half out of the closet in cowboy boots. Alas, my husband crashed the dress rehearsal, saying the cowboy boots were hell and the dress should go to jumble immediately. After much borrowing I unearthed a white flimsy dress, which he agreed was more suitable.

Monday was spent gathering accessories: several necklaces, three scarves to knot pirate fashion round my waist, the first bra I'd bought in ten years (that was a shock – I'd swelled from 36B to a massive 80B cup), a pair of black sling-backs, and some moccasins, unaccountably called 'Socrates'. I thought I had prepared for every eventuality.

Ascot day dawned below zero, with force-ten gales and not enough blue sky outside even to make a pair of Prince Andrew's trousers. Not only would I freeze in my white dress, but, putting it on in daylight, I discovered two vast white pockets hanging down towards my groin like obscene kidneys. At this rate, I sobbed, I would reach Ascot wearing only my straw hat, like an Italian donkey. The sole alternative was an ancient black-belted tent. Topped by my hat, I looked like a wedding above the neck, and a fat funeral below. A scratched midge bite on my ankle wept through my black tights in sympathy.

Adrian George, who was coming along to illustrate the piece, had also never been to Ascot. Getting kitted up he hadn't fared much better. His car had been towed away after four hours' queuing at Moss Bros, and they had persuaded him into a grey top hat not big enough to trap a rat. He kept tucking his morning coat into his trousers thinking it was shirt-tails. Irritatingly, both he and my husband looked infinitely more glamorous than me.

Happily we'd been invited to lunch in a box on the top tier, where the view of the Ascot Course unrolls like those double-page spreads in a Babar book. Below, coloured hats and grey toppers swarmed around the bookies – a psychedelic mushroom farm. The band played Gilbert and Sullivan. Helicopters like great birds landed in a distant field laying precious cargoes of jockeys. To the left, heels sinking into the Royal Enclosure grass indicated the sawftness of the going. In the distance fluffy green woods had been washed and fabric-conditioned by weeks of rain.

And if I looked frightful, a lot of people looked almost as bad. The Jut Set – well endowed girls in very low-cut dresses – were out in force. Others, determined to wear their flimsiest dresses, topped them with short fur coats, looking rather like our senior cat when he had a nervous breakdown and went bald below the waist.

Lady Diana's influence was paramount. Girl after girl sported the short white off-the-shoulder replica of the famous black taffeta she wore to the Lord Mayor's Dinner. Gooseflesh turning purple beneath four layers of Man Tan, they displayed bright orange elbows, each time they clutched their hats in the icy wind. Not that I was faring much better — my hat elastic snapped at the first gust.

After a glass or two of champagne, however, I began to cheer up. Even gulls' eggs were worn off-the-shoulder this year — a thoughtful waitress had peeled the shell off the tops. Gradually other guests appeared in the box. I was slightly startled when a sauve gentleman produced a pair of tights out of his handbag. 'They're mine,' explained the woman he came with. 'One *must* take spare tights to Ascot, in case they get laddered by umbrellas.'

Next to arrive was a wonderful blonde in a dashing shocking-pink hat.

'My hats have much more fun in life than I do,' she sighed. 'This one's coming every day this week on different girlfriends.'

'Rather like jockeys,' said my husband looking visibly impressed.

As the time for the Queen's arrival approached, the tension mounted. Policemen faced outwards, as crowds thickly lined the rails. Welcome light relief was provided by a huge yellow penguin, a pink kangaroo, and a blue rabbit, which were perched on a rail among the jellied eel stalls across the track.

'They're security guards,' said a fat woman in an adjacent box knowledgeably. 'Well perhaps they're not,' she went on, as the rabbit's head fell off.

The loveliest sight in England must be the Queen and her convoy of carriages coming like an arrow up the emerald-green track, past the cheap stands and the captains of industry in their boxes, past the Royal Enclosure, and turning left through an avenue of raised toppers and pretty bobbing ladies to that heart of the establishment, the Royal Box. Nowhere is the Queen more popular than on the race track (and never more so than after her display of pluck and *sang-froid* when someone fired blanks at her at the Trooping of the Colour). Not since I saw Domingo take a curtain call at Covent Garden, have

I heard the cheers and bravos ring out more tumultuously.

The Queen was followed by a foxglove-pink blob that was Princess Margaret, and a Parma-violet blob, which someone said was Lady Diana. No one however could miss Princess Michael, her ebullient wave rotating on all sides like a windmill.

One of life's minor humiliations is having to move other people's binoculars inwards because one's eyes are closer set. Minor, however, compared with the humiliation of the poor man in the next-door box, who was close to tears because he'd provided a lavish lunch for twenty, and no one had showed up.

Whatever has been said about the riff-raff of parvenus and ex-jailbirds who have recently infiltrated the Royal Enclosure, I thought the people in there looked splendid. From our box, you could see that the colours of the women's dresses were far more sharp and vibrant than those in the public stands: brilliant reds and fuchsias, gentian blues and dusty pinks, all set off by the black and grey of the morning coats and top hats. The women's skirts were worn as they have been for the last twenty years, bang on the knee. Only here too were hats staying on without being held. Are the women's heads so hard from falling off ponies in their youth, that they don't feel the hat pins?

The men looked equally glamorous. It being the first day, their morning coats hadn't had time to get creased. Most had the sort of lean figures where you couldn't tell if they'd been to Moss Bros until they lifted their race glasses. One is reminded of Wilfred Hyde-White's exquisite pre-war comment on Hitler: 'If the fellow's going to raise his arm so much, he really ought to go to a decent tailor.'

In answer to everyone's question – Lady Diana is infinitely more gorgeous in the flesh. I didn't get near her at Ascot, but at a garden party a few weeks ago, she was only a couple of feet away. Above all you remember the dazzlingly direct speedwell-blue gaze – like Polly in *Love in a Cold Climate*. But there is also a combination of sweetness, shyness and peachy voluptuousness reminiscent of the youthful Lillie Langtry.

Her impact on fashion has been so dramatic and widespread, she might even persuade upper-class women at last to abandon their bare foreheads and Alice-banded hair for the far more flattering fringe which shades yet emphasizes the eyes like a big-brimmed hat.

Over in the paddock, only the keys shed by the lime tree marred the striped perfection of the grass. Out came the jockeys in their rainbow silks.

'Aren't they pretty?' said a girl in a rose courtelle.

'Bit small,' said her friend. 'I like a man to be tall.'

'I'm going to back that one,' said a braless blonde in ketchup red, 'because of his lovely long legs.'

'Sure you're talking about the horses?' asked her boyfriend acidly.

Walking across the grass, one constantly avoided being run down by people bucketing past in wheelchairs, presumably recovering from riding and skiing accidents. One very old man, however, was careering after his ancient wife like Steve McQueen in *Bullitt*. 'Poor thing's lorst her memory,' he bellowed, reversing sharply into an acquaintance. 'Keeps thinkin' she's married to someone else.'

Everywhere people were saying how well Mrs Thatcher was doing.

'Except for unemployment – poor dear,' said a horse-faced woman.

'I'm sure if they changed the word Dole to Arts Council Grant,' drawled a young exquisite, 'no one would feel it a *bit* infra dig to be out of work.'

One could imagine a lefty at Ascot hacking his way through such a dense jungle of conservatism and falling on another lefty's neck, thankfully crying: 'Kenneth Livingstone, I presume.'

Later I passed three amazing girls, one with a stuffed

71

telephone on her head, another with a stuffed ice-cream cornet, and a third with a stuffed iron with a flex wound round and round, and a three-point plug hanging down the back like a Davy Crockett tail.

Back at our box, the man who'd been in tears next door had cheered up noticeably because his friends – chiefly top brass from the clearing banks – had finally turned up. My husband viewed them in horror: 'I'd have cried much harder when they arrived,' he said. Adrian George was in transports, having won £90 on the last race. At least it'd pay for his car being towed away.

Perhaps the nicest part of the day was that instead of bolting home after the last race, people all hung over the backs of their boxes, and watched the crowds gathering round the bandstands and dancing to the music. A frantic Charleston with morning-coat tails flying was followed by a decorous waltz, then by a sing-song. No one could accuse the English of coldness, as in an orgy of patriotism, tears streaking the women's mascara, they belted out 'There'll Always be an England'.

'Rule Britannia' next, and the fact that a woman in a wheelchair as high as a kite was conducting the crowd in a completely different tempo to the bandmaster, only added to the general jollity. In the tiers below all you could see were waving Union Jacks and coloured hats like window boxes of sweet peas. 'Jerusalem', then 'Land of Hope and Glory', 'Roll out the Barrel' (double presumably), and then the National Anthem. There must have been a lump in every throat, as we roared out:

> Send her Victorious,
> Happy and Glorious
> *Long* to reign over us

– and really meant it.

On reflection, it seems a pity there's so much hysteria about the lobster-and-champagne aspect of Ascot, when you merely have people of all classes enjoying a vintage day out. Most of them only come on one day, and have probably saved up for the treat all year. And at least my legs enjoyed their first day of freedom.

This little pig went a-marketing

I was signing paperbacks in a shop the other day when the manageress started talking about Angela Rippon's first children's book. After she'd raved about the publicity material for several minutes, I asked her what the book was like. 'I haven't bothered to read it,' she said dismissively. 'With Angela's name on it, anything will sell.'

Partly to convince myself that publishing hadn't been totally corrupted by the media, I spent five days at the Children's Book Fair in Bologna. An added incentive was that my husband, who was then working for Frederick Warne, publishers of Beatrix Potter, was also going. Perhaps I'd be left in charge of the Warne stand, and dazzle everyone by selling Samuel Whiskers to the Latvians.

The plane out was packed with publishers – mostly women. With their jersey dresses, coloured stockings, and well-cut unstreaked hair, they were more elegant than female dons, but retained a slightly academic air. Drabble rather than drab. Upper-middle-class voices rang out. One sees why mothers like their daughters to go into publishing, particularly the children's department where there's no chance of bumping into people like Harold Robbins.

The men looked more battered. It's been a grim year for the trade. Not a member of the staff fired in anger, but some heartbreaking redundancies; anyone lucky enough to be in work is doing three people's jobs.

After take-off, Captain Alice welcomed us aboard, which was appropriate since we were flying into a gastronomic wonderland, home of spaghetti bolognese. Arriving at Bologna, a swarthy French publisher had his portfolio ripped open by customs, who seemed disap-

74

pointed only to find coloured illustrations of bears playing football.

Up at dawn next morning to set up the stand. Despite being a cradle of hedonism, Bologna is run by the Communists. To reach the fair you somewhat bizarrely pass the Cicisbeo Hotel, the Crest Motel, and the Via Stalingrad – next stop Siberia. Soon we were blu-tacking posters of Ginger and Pickles and Tabitha Twitchit to the walls, and unpacking plastic models of Jemima Puddle-duck.

Other publishers were blowing up balloons, and hanging up mobiles of cucumbers in baseball caps. Down the aisle, Babar was celebrating his fiftieth birthday; Pinocchio, now a hundred, had an exhibition to himself. In the next hall, a large notice announced 'Humorous strips for children'. Could Rupert Bear be going to remove his check trousers at last?

Inevitably there were disasters. One publisher hadn't ordered any furniture. One beautiful editor was in despair because her chivalrous boss, insisting on carrying her suitcase, had absentmindedly left it behind at Gatwick. The Macmillan contingent, attempting to cut costs, had driven with all the stock over the Alps and been hijacked by an avalanche.

'I've got a monstrous great video screen, and nothing to play tapes on,' screamed a publisher, who, because of a telly spin-off, was hoping to justify a first printing of 300,000.

Wandering round the fair, one was assaulted by primary colours. The rainbow didn't come and go here, it blazed all the time. Following the trend of today's television plays, children's books were heavily into urgent contemporary themes. There was fiction for five-year-olds on coping with homosexuality, bedwetting, epileptic sisters, mongol brothers. Althea of Dinosaur had an excellent new picture book explaining the workings of the unions, and another suggesting how you'll feel as a five-year-old when your parents split up.

The other eternal children's book theme is anthropo-morphism, the difficulty being to find a new animal to write about. Ernest Benn have introduced some fantastic subterranean hippos called the Trumpets, Jeffrey Archer has a killer kipper. The Canadians have retaliated with a bestseller about an ant-eater who falls in love with an ant. Hodders of Australia have managed to combine animals and urgent contemporary themes by producing a book called *The Latch-Key Dog*.

The most important thing at a trade fair is to look busy all the time, activity attracting activity. As soon as anyone visits your stand, you mop your brow, and say 'It's quite amazing, you've caught me at the first quiet moment today'. Nor at a publishing fair are there any of those smouldering departure-lounge eye-meets leading to liaisons which agreeably pass the time at normal trade fairs. The only wolves to be found, in fact, were on the covers of the children's books on the Russian stand. All the better to eat up the West, my dear.

Outer space and comics dominated the American sector, whose worst lapse in taste was a strip-cartoon book of the New Testament with Christ on the cross with a balloon coming out of his mouth. The same publishers have also sold half-a-million copies of the *Christian Mother Goose*.

> Humpty Dumpty sat on a wall,
> Humpty Dumpty had a great fall,
> Humpty Dumpty shouted Amen.
> God will put me together again.

On one French stand, it was nice to see a woman editor with silvery hair drawn into a bun, ignoring all the hyping and gesticulating around her, and quietly reading *Père Goriot*. Returning to the Warne stand, I found that *Teddy Bear Coalman* had been sold to the Japs, and I'd missed a squawking match with Gallimard over the pricing of *Peter Rabbit*.

Peter Ustinov, who was supposed to open the fair at five o'clock, had been delayed by the Oscars which had been postponed because of the Reagan shooting, but was expected to make the prize-giving banquet later that night.

Utterly exhausted, we trailed out into the Bologna sunshine at the end of the day. If the competition was gentle inside the hall, it was extremely fierce outside. One full-bosomed English girl had already climbed into a taxi, when she was firmly lifted out and dumped on the pavement by a steely-eyed German publisher who felt she was queue barging.

Off to the banquet. Bologna at night is intensely theatrical. Beneath an indigo sky, huge floodlit arches, great studded doors, leaning towers, and terracotta squares succeed each other like operatic sets. Even the endlessly peripatetic Italians form naturally into crowd scenes. Verdi roars out of every brick.

Inside the *palazzo*, the vice-president of the fair, urbane as the Count in *Figaro*, praised the high standard of the entries, which can only lead to the 'batterment' of children's books. The adult jury had given first prize to a foul series of books featuring a Swiss television character in a vast red hat called Yok Yok.

The children's jury happily had better taste and chose an English book by Jenny Partridge about a mole shoemaker called Mr Squint. 'We liked the book,' they said in their report, 'because the animal characters are dressed like we are, move like us, do the same work, and want the same things.' Which is exactly what Beatrix Potter and Kenneth Grahame were doing seventy years ago – so nothing has changed.

Banquet time – and the unedifying sight of the world's publishers, all on expense accounts, clawing and fighting their way into an exquisite renaissance hall, and beneath a blaze of chandeliers falling on the most beautiful food I've ever seen. Huge cornucopias of fish fantastically decorated with shells and lobsters, haunches of ham sequinned all over with jellied cucumber slices, sucking pigs daisied with hard-boiled eggs, were soon being ripped apart. Fingers scrabbled at the vast dark chocolate ramparts of Pinocchio's birthday cake.

After half an hour the guzzling slowed, and a whispering of "e is 'ere, 'e is 'ere' grew into a great roar. Poor Peter Ustinov, finally arrived, was apologizing for being late. He looked rumpled, forlorn and very, very tired. I was reminded of Paddington arriving in London. I wanted to rush up and hang a note round his neck saying 'Please look after this bear'. The Italians obviously felt the same. Next minute he disappeared behind a swarm of dark-suited dignitaries.

Day merged into day. Outside the *primavera* was raging. It was unbearable each morning to exchange all that pink and white blossom and acid-green burgeoning for the foetid prison of the exhibition hall. After a leaden start, however, business was picking up. On the Kestrel stand, Tony Lacey was waving a telegram: 'The Australians are prepared to take 32,000 copies if we take out the reference to farting on page 16.'

The girl on the Hodder stand countered with a cable from her dog: 'Come back at once. Where's supper?' The beautiful girl who'd lost her suitcase was looking miserable after four days in the same blue sweater. Most of the lady publishers had abandoned their jersey dresses in favour of folk-weave smocks to accommodate the pasta spread.

Great attention was being focused this year on the pre-school group. Mitchell Beazely had a glossy new 24-book encyclopaedia, a do-it-yourself prodigy kit, called *Learning Together*.

'The child looks at the big coloured picture book,' a salesman was explaining, 'while the mother asks it questions from the small book. You can do it while you're ironing, just put the small book on your ironing board.'

Perhaps *Scorching Together* would be a better title.

Last day. Despite having small Jemima Puddleduck eyes
from exhaustion and shooting off buttons from overeat-
ing like Tom Kitten, everyone was feeling pleasantly end-
of-termish. Books were being packed. People were giving
parties to finish up bottles. An editor on the Hodder stand
had become a grandfather and was dispensing champagne. The poor girl with no clothes was wearing someone else's pyjama top, and nervously asking people if she
smelt. An impossibly handsome Greek publisher was
flipping through a picture book on the Dinosaur stand:
'What ees thees Heekory Deekory Dock? Ees no good for
Greece.'

I had a quick look at the Pinocchio exhibition. How
patrician, austere and storklike was the original Pinocchio — not unlike the young Charles de Gaulle. How
vulgar by comparison seems the Disney version with his
huge Bambi eyes and Tyrolean hat. Yet by vulgarizing
him, Disney immortalized him, resulting in millions of
children returning to the original book. Perhaps one
shouldn't worry about corruption by the media.

On the way to the airport, a taxi driver told us the
Children's Book Fair was totally different from any other
trade fair held in Bologna because the brothels were
always empty. The prostitutes, he went on, warming to
his subject, always went on holiday this week, but they
were already drifting back for the Engineers' Fair next
week.

Brighton or bust

I've never been a keen motorist. I don't drive, I tend to get sick, and my least favourite sentence in the world is: 'Shall we take the longer way round, it's so much prettier?' It was with extreme trepidation, therefore, that I accepted Lady Montagu's invitation to drive on the Brighton Run with her one Sunday.

Nor is rising at 5.30 a.m. my idea of heaven. But fuelled by a splendid breakfast of kidneys and scrambled eggs at the Royal Lancaster Hotel, I began to perk up. Soon other Beaulieu competitors wandered in, rubbing sleep out of their eyes, including Monsieur and Madame Panhard, Lord Montagu, Sterling Moss, followed by Prince Michael of Kent, looking the image of George V in his new beard.

My own glamorous driver, Fiona Montagu, was wearing a leather coat and hat trimmed with fur. Dreading a cold day, I had planned my clothes for an arctic expedition. I ended up more like a theatre programme in a splendid floor-length wolf coat courtesy of Lord Montagu, a fox hat courtesy of Mrs William Franklyn and thermal underwear courtesy of Woolworths.

I'd tried on the thermal underwear the night before. Thinking I looked rather sexy, I cavorted into the sitting room to show my husband, who'd promptly clapped his hands over his eyes, groaning that he'd never expected to have a wife who looked like a postal ad in *The Lady*.

My thermals plus the hotel central heating turned my face as scarlet as the rose of Lancaster. So despite hellish nerves, I was relieved when we all surged out to our cars. Ours was a little Progress built in 1901. For an octogenarian, she looked very sprightly with her ruby-red paintwork, gleaming brass lamps and flat mushroom of a steering wheel rising from the floor.

Ashley Dunne, the Beaulieu mechanic, a genial blond giant more like a basket-ball player, was giving the car a last polish. In fur and trembling, I scrambled in beside Fiona Montagu.

'If it doesn't start,' she said, 'Ashley will give us a tickle.'

It didn't. Ashley plunged his hand into the bowels of the engine, and off we went charging terrifyingly down the slope of the car-park ramp straight through a red light into Bayswater Road.

'It's hectic when it's wet like this, because the brakes don't work,' explained Fiona calmly, as we belted into Hyde Park, removing buttons from several policemen's tunics before joining the three hundred veteran cars in the starting area.

'Tonight, my arm muscles will really seize up,' she went on, jamming on the brakes with both hands, leaving the steering wheel to its own devices and sending a group of spectators leaping for their lives.

'Could one of you give us a push into our parking lot?' she called out. 'I'm afraid we can't reverse.'

Instantly a swarm of eager-beavers in flat caps and Hush Puppies leapt to our aid. Only fifty-seven miles to Brighton, I thought faintly, too late to back out now. Thank God we were having a coffee break at Gatwick. All around us, women in poke bonnets and men in deerstalkers were hysterically revving, winding up and polishing their cars. In their gusto and exhibitionism they reminded one of the audience in *The Good Old Days*.

Prince Michael came over to wish us God speed. His arrival had been almost as hazardous as ours.

'I took a right turn and got lorst in Shepherd's Bush, then broke down on the way back, rather ignominous.'

Travelling as his passenger was his nephew James Ogilvy, who was so outstandingly good-looking that all the pretty girls were vying to ogle him.

81

In clouds of smoke, the leaders were going down to the start. The Serpentine writhed greyly in the gentle breeze. Red setters bounding in the damp tawny leaves, a chestnut police horse, children in yellow gumboots, all enhanced the golden beauty of the park.

'Look thy last on all things lovely,' I muttered through chattering teeth, as we bucketed off to the start, endangering the lives of several photographers.

'Check the oil every three miles,' called Ashley.

'Our Father which art in heaven,' I pleaded silently, oblivious of the cheering crowds and the television cameras.

'It gives one such a feeling of power having all the traffic held up for one,' cried Fiona, as we careered on two wheels round Hyde Park Corner, and shooting several more red lights set off towards Westminster Bridge.

'I can smell burning,' I squeaked, as a crowd of Texans whooped past us in a cloud of steam.

'Not us,' said Fiona soothingly. 'Never look behind, it only makes one nervous. Anyway I can't see a thing in my rear mirror, it shakes too much.'

In Dean Farrar Street, we passed two disconsolate drivers, whose car had broken down. Lucky things, I thought disloyally. But gradually, as we swept past the green dome of the Imperial War Museum, and the crowds huddling in deck-chairs on the leaf-strewn pavements of Kennington, my competitive spirit began to rally.

'Move, you ugly brute,' I found myself shouting at a bus which wouldn't let us pass.

'Beastly modern car,' wailed Fiona, as we were overtaken by a car only a year younger than Progress.

We had now left the breed dogs of central London behind, and moved into the mongrel country of Streatham and Norbury. All along the route, in fact, were thousands of dogs, most of them with their backs to the road, probably in a sulk because their owners were taking so much interest in the cars.

The wind was getting up now. Fiona adjusted her hat with both hands, and nearly ran into a bread van.

'Road Hog,' I howled, having now completely accepted that Progress had divine right of way over all other vehicles. Even an ambulance going by on tow didn't destroy my confidence.

Entering Surrey, Ashley and my husband caught us up in the back-up car. Described in the programme as a 'tender vehicle', I was afraid it soon would be, with all the veteran cars bumping into it. My husband said it was a nightmare following behind us. With me constantly pointing out dogs, and Fiona describing the private lives of mutual friends, random hand signals were whizzing out to left and right like one of those multi-armed Indian love gods. We were so busy gassing, we took a wrong turn at Croydon, and had to do a U-turn, bringing an army of oncoming traffic to a screeeching halt. 'Trust a woman', guffawed a spectator.

As we moved deeper into Surrey, mongrels gave way to breed dogs again. Colonels in huskies replaced men in anoraks. Boarding kennels took over from bingo halls. We had a tense moment at a Redhill crossroads, when a milk float went slap across our path and refused to stop. If looks could curdle.

As the two girls rode past on palamino horses, an orange aeroplane rose out of the amber trees. Ahead at last lay Gatwick.

'Shall we stop for coffee?' asked Fiona.

'No, No,' I cried, blood thoroughly up now. 'Onward to Brighton.'

Apart from the magical countryside and the fresh air, I was really turned on by the enthusiasm of the crowds, who cheered and waved all along the route. I was soon waving back at absolutely everyone, convinced they'd be hurt if I didn't. Megalomania was setting in fast. A major irritation were the flocks of bicyclists pedalling in perfect formation, who kept cashing in on our slipstream. I longed to whip them away like a charioteer. I was getting more like Mr Toad every minute.

Now we entered the chalklands of Sussex, flashing past ploughed fields and woods dipped in henna. Pink hydrangeas turned to blue in the cottage gardens. Only thirteen miles to Brighton, the traffic was thickening alarmingly. Turning a corner we were faced by two solid crawling lines of traffic. Ashley was nowhere to be seen. If we stalled in this lot, we might have to wait hours for him to catch up and give us a tickle. But my brave insouciant companion was not to be daunted: 'I'm going to create a middle line,' she cried imperiously. 'Roads are always wider than one thinks,' and approaching at a brisk 25 m.p.h. she drove slap through the two traffic lines. Gallant Progress responded like Stroller. Chicken Cooper closed her eyes in terror till we were out the other end.

On we surged passing broken-down cars with hoots of unsympathetic laughter like Kenneth More in *Genevieve*. The crowds were still growing, gathering round pubs as midday approached. There can't be much wrong with England, I kept thinking, when it produces enthusiasm like this, particularly when it's directed at me.

Nemesis descended swiftly. Progress started to falter and backfire. I couldn't bear it. I'd die if we didn't reach Brighton. But next minute we ground to a sickening halt on the edge of a copse, ironically festooned with traveller's joy. Two men gabbling Dutch leapt to our assistance, but to no avail.

'Ashley, we need you,' we wailed with all the fervour of Scarlet O'Hara.

Five agonizing minutes later, the back-up car came round the corner. Ashley eyed the gabbling Dutchmen.

'You've come a long way, Lady M.,' he said sardonically. 'The locals talk funny round here.'

For a further agonizing ten minutes, he fiddled with knobs and wires, and then as a last resort changed our only spark plug. We clambered back in again. The little car coughed, spluttered, backfired, then, rallying to the goodwill of the crowd, set off again. Seagulls and helicopters circled above us like vultures, but ahead lay the misty hills behind Brighton. It was like *Pilgrim's Progress*. Might we make the heavenly city after all?

'Difficult to do four things at once,' murmured Fiona, as she tried to steer, brake, stay in neutral and keep up the revs. Then suddenly, almost without realizing it, we passed the pylons, two stone monoliths marking the boundaries of the city. And the trumpets sounded for us on the other side.

Now there was no stopping us. In a haze of euphoria we shot into Brighton – Bright Town with the elm trees raining red-gold leaves on to our heads. Shooting several more lights, we hurtled straight for the sea, just managing to swing left along the packed sea-front – the first of the Beaulieu competitors to clock in – taking just over 3½ hours. As we proudly chugged over the finishing line, I had to be forcibly restrained from plunging into the cheering crowds and going on a walkabout.

Spitting out wolf fur, like the senior dog after a fight, I bid a fond farewell to gallant Progress, looking as trim and shiningly ruby-red as when we started. I wanted to give her a bran mash and a rub down. After all for a few hours she had allowed me to feel like a Princess.

Learning the
hard way

The cruel C.E.

This is an account of what is believed to be a unique educational experiment which took place in the spring of 1981.

On Monday 8 June, thousands of prep-school boys all over the country will begin probably the first really harrowing ordeal of their lives. They will be taking Common Entrance – or C.E. as it's known – an exam they must pass to get into the public school of their parents' choice. The exam is spread over four days with a maximum of fifteen hours of papers, including French, Latin, Greek, Science, and three Maths papers which would unsettle the most senior Wrangler.

The little examinees are by no means the only people biting their nails. So are their parents and the prep-school heads who stake their reputation on how many pupils make it. To make matters worse, candidates can't play the field and try several schools simultaneously. If little Charles ploughs Eton, where his family have been for generations, only then can his papers be handed on to another less academically demanding school. Even if this second school takes him, which is no means certain, it is likely that Granny who has set her heart on Eton, may not now be prepared to flog the last of the silver to help pay the fees. Pressures on candidates to pass are, therefore, from all quarters, colossal.

Being an interested party, having a son at prep school who is already grumbling darkly about taking C.E. in a year's time, and having been bored rigid at countless dinner parties by neurotic mothers describing their C.E. traumas, I thought it would be illuminating to ask a team of illustrious grown-ups to take some of the last year's papers under strict exam conditions and see how they fared.

The final line-up who accepted my invitation were: the newly ennobled Lord Beloff; A. J. P. Taylor; Ludovic Kennedy; Brian Inglis; our own Godfrey Smith; Frank Muir, who despite his dazzling erudition left school at fourteen and claims to have never taken an exam in his life; Joanna Lumley; Susan Stranks, who went to four different schools ending up at Mrs Hampshire's Dancing School; and myself. A pretty catholic bunch. The only common denominator was that the other candidates, at least, were all secure enough not to mind making complete idiots of themselves.

Finding a day when everyone was free was a bit like putting on a stage play. We settled for Monday the 13th. Westminster School kindly lent us a classroom. I chose one lined with ancient copies of Pliny and Sophocles, which had been built over the site of the original monastic dungeons, and which had chairs far enough apart to enable the candidates not to cheat. As we had only one day, it was decided just to take Scripture, History, Maths I, French II, Geography and English Comprehension.

The night before the exam, my son got into an understandable panic that I'd fail and offered to coach me in Maths. Instead I took his Scripture exercise book to bed. The first essay on the birth of Christ was all about the 'sky being filled with angles', which sounded more like geometry. Turning the page, I read that 'Goliarth was a philistine giant three metres high', and gave up.

C.E. dawned absolutely arctic. Earth had a great deal to show more fair than Westminster Bridge blocked solid with traffic. Examinees were coming from all over the country – would they ever m..ke it on time?

Under disapproving grey skies, the russet Westminster courtyard had lost all its warmth. The double sherry shivering in the icy wind could not have looked more forlorn than Susan Stranks, the first candidate to clock in, her bright pink dungarees emphasizing a face as white as blackboard chalk.

No, she felt too sick for coffee, and did I think they'd

have a question on the Roman conquest? Husband Robin Ray had been coaching her all night. A. J. P. Taylor arrived next, a small indomitable figure in a deerstalker. He reminds one of an irreverent mole who delights in pushing up molehills to disturb the smooth green lawns of conventional historical thought. He was followed by another distinguished historian, Max Beloff, who'd been brave enough to wear his All Souls' tie. Then came Frank Muir in a black schoolboy cap towering over them both – a very unphilistine giant two metres high.

'What a terrible idea,' he moaned, rolling his R's balefully. 'Why on earth are we all here?'

Collective disenchantment was increased by Ludovic

QUESTION: Describe the events surrounding the birth of Jesus as seen through the eyes of the inn-keeper.

FRANK MUIR: Well, the authorities, bless 'em decided to hold a big nationwide census in our little town of Bethlehem — an absolute God-send to us of the Bethlehem Chamber of Commerce and Round Table — and the lady wife and I got stuck in cleaning up the old inn, washing a few of the dirtier sheets, watering the wine and other professional chores ... Then, if you please, along comes this pair of peasants from some hick village called Nazareth. 'A room, please, landlord,' he calls, bold as brass, as though it was a wet weekend in Feb. and the inn was empty. Seems the girl was very preggers so the wife let them sit in the warm for a bit ... I reckoned they were trouble-makers and I was right. Soon my stable was a-wash with greasy shepherds dropping cheese and pie and other rubbish into the straw. And some concert party, or pop group, called The Three Kings cluttered up the place with their groupies — the girl gave birth to a lad. Often wonder what became of him.

Kennedy, glamorous in a pin-striped suit, who'd just come out of hospital, and Brian Inglis, feeling possibly even frailer, after an assault-course weekend of Dublin hospitality. Finally our own Godfrey Smith shambled in, for once not his usual jolly self.

Big Ben tolled the hour. As it was essential that the examinees should be marked anonymously, they were asked to put a number rather than their name at the top of the page. Trembling with nerves, I passed out the Scripture papers. There followed a stunned, horrified silence. Then Frank Muir rose to his feet.

'I'm off, chaps,' he said. 'I've already got a place at Guildford Grammar.'

Everyone collapsed into giggles, and, very tentatively, pens started to move over the lined paper. Soon coats were removed; Frank whipped off his pink bow tie. Godfrey's gusty sighs were ruffling everyone's papers.

'Some of us are trying to work, Smith,' said Frank tartly.

A. J. P. was writing steadily, stopping every so often to shake with helpless laughter. Everyone else was tearing their hair. Few of us in fact would have escaped the scissors of the school barber. He'd have certainly hacked off Ludo's pin-striped locks, had an inch of Smith and Inglis, and at least a foot off Cooper.

Big Ben told us time was up.

'Please Miss,' piped up the irrepressible Muir, 'Kennedy's cheating, he's still writing.'

'Just finishing my sentence,' said Ludo airily, carrying on sub-clausing down the page, with almost Proustian felicity.

'How do you spell "myrrh"?' asked Muir of the room at large.

'M-U-I-R,' came back Ludo, quick as a flash, as he handed in his paper.

On to History, which I found stymingly difficult, but which at least had some questions where you could waffle

92

like 'Write a letter home to your mother describing a journey on the Royal Mail Coach'.

Despite initial groaning, reminiscent of a labour ward in the rush hour, everyone was happier now. Beloff, Taylor, Inglis, Muir, Kennedy and Smith had already written whole books in answer to many of the questions. The problem was what to leave out, or they'd still be finishing the paper next year. Most candidates used to typewriters were suffering from writer's cramp. 'Slaving over a hot IBM is nothing to this,' grumbled Max Beloff, waving his fingers like a typist drying her nails.

Once again Big Ben told us time had run out.

'Never send to know for whom the bell tolls,' intoned Muir lugubriously.

Everyone fell on the elevenses' champagne, which seemed more fitting than school milk.

'Who are those two distinguished-looking actors coming across the courtyard?' whispered my secretary.

They turned out to be Michael and John Farebrother, headmasters of St Peter's School, Seaford, who manage miraculously to maintain a sense of humour while running a very successful prep school. They had nobly agreed to mark our papers, and invigilate Maths and French. By a strange coincidence, Mike Farebrother and Ludo discovered they'd once played in a jazz group at Oxford with Humphrey Lyttleton, and were soon remembering a gig at the W.I. at which they strummed away for four hours, sustained only by tea and rock buns.

By an even stranger coincidence, Godfrey said, when he was taking his degree at Oxford, Max Beloff had been the invigilator. 'The candidate in front of me was scattering sweet papers as he wrote,' said Godfrey. 'Max, always a stickler for law and order, insisted he pick them up. The candidate, Michael Drummond, is now Wykeham Professor of Logic at Oxford.'

We all agreed that the exams so far had been incredibly difficult, particularly for small boys, but buoyed up by several glasses of champagne on empty stomachs, we now felt quite sanguine about taking Maths I. It turned out to be a stinker, reducing the whole room to hysterics. Suddenly an ear-splitting explosion shook the corridor outside. 'Beloff's shot himself,' said Muir.

But it was only another bottle being opened. Totally non-plussed by a geometry question, I was just praying that some angles might appear out of the sky, when there was a commotion in the courtyard outside. On investigation it turned out to be an unctuous cleric in a black cassock guiding a party of blue-rinsed Americans over the school. He was only just deflected from sweeping them into our classroom. Imagine the letters back to Iowa:

'Dearest Elmer, Today we visited a darling antique British public school in London, England. Even the boys are antiques there, Elmer, and they have liquor and girls in the classroom. No wonder Britain is going to the dogs.'

We were wrestling with an impossible question about crumpets costing x pence per dozen, when any serious

QUESTION: What advantage is it to the UK if North Sea oil is sold to other countries?
A. J. P. TAYLOR: Cash intake – you imbecile.

attempts at work were totally sabotaged by the very uncommon entrance of Joanna Lumley, ravishingly dressed as a schoolboy. In the final week of rehearsing *Private Lives*, in which she played Amanda, she'd only been allowed off for an hour to take a quick Math's paper and pose for the group photograph. Later she was going to do the exams under strict supervision at home.

'I can't remember what paper I'm taking,' wailed Brian Inglis.

'Probably something about the effects of alcohol on small boys,' said Ludo.

A. J. P. gave up at this juncture, content to gaze instead at Joanna's emerald-green back.

'Not too bored?' I whispered.

'Not nearly as bored as I would be if I were doing the paper,' he replied.

Maths despatched, we all lined up for the group photo. We had reached the silly stage of paper darts and itching powder. The photographer had great difficulty stopping Brian Inglis running round the back to get in the picture twice. Next we movedon to lunch at Locketts, haunt of cabinet ministers. Conversation was very high table. 'I told the examiners they'd spelt Pearl Harbor wrong,' said A.J.P. with evident satisfaction, plunging his spoon into some seafood cocktail. I talked to Michael Farebrother (who before becoming a headmaster, had coached Prince Charles) about the pressures endured by boys taking C.E.

'They go round as if under hypnosis until they get the results,' he said. 'We had one very quiet, undemonstrative boy a few years ago. When I called him in to tell him he'd passed, he suddenly started to shout and shout, then he flung his arms round me, and when I extricated myself, he started shouting again.'

On another occasion, Michael had been walking down the passage after lights out, and, hearing noises coming

---

QUESTION: Tell in your own words what happened during Elijah's stay in the house of the widow.

FRANK MUIR: It has been a matter of rumour and gossip ever since. The Scripture gives one version. The version based on local gossip is too vile to repeat. In my view exactly what occurred between Elijah and the widow should be left in the decent obscurity of the New English Bible.

---

from one of the dormitories, had tiptoed closer and peered in. All the little boys were kneeling down, and the somewhat overbearing dormitory captain was whispering fiercely: 'While you're all saying your prayers, you might like to remember I'm taking C.E. on Monday.'

Meanwhile down the table, John Farebrother was regaling everyone with C.E. howlers.

'Queen Elizabeth knitted Sir Walter Raleigh on the deck,' one boy had written, to which the examiner had added: 'Presumably into Lord Cardigan.'

My favourite was 'When Mary heard she was to be the mother of Jesus, she went off and sang the Magna Carta'.

Back to the classroom, and French II. The day was taking on a dreamlike quality. John Farebrother read out the dictation twice in his sepulchral English Milor French, and earned a round of applause from all the candidates. French was pretty easy – for some. Geography on the other hand was a brute, with an incomprehensible Ordnance Survey map, and impossible questions about oil rigs and the third world. This was, on the other hand, one of the few papers which seemed to have dragged itself into the eighties.

A quick champagne break was followed by the last paper English Comprehension, which I finished in a canter because I omitted to turn the page and do all the compulsory questions on the other side. Everyone else did very well, although some examinees' writing, I noticed, was blurred by drink rings – talk about the wine-dark C.E. The last candidate put down her pen.

It had been a magnificent day, which probably worked because we all dreaded it, and because everyone rose so splendidly to the occasion. I have never been more tired in my life (and we'd only done a third of the papers) but I was very proud of my team, as they staggered exhausted out of Westminster. They all reported falling asleep like puppies the moment they got home. Except for A. J. P. who trotted off to the tube as sprightly as a lark.

'Next year,' was his parting shot, 'We'll all take finals.'

Schoolboys taking C.E. often have to wait a fortnight to get their results. The noble Farebrothers took the papers back to Seaford, and returned them in under a week. Scripture came back first and was quite hilarious, although most of the candidates would probably have ended up in the monastic dungeons for blasphemy. Here is Frank Muir on how St Peter escaped from prison, as described by one of the screws:

I padlocked Peter to the wall; at that moment he began to cry.
'What ails thee, prisoner?' I cried.
'Nosebleed, sir,' he responded. 'Could I have a bit of cold metal to put down my back?'
Looking back, sir, I felt I made my big mistake there, I gave him the key.

More people did well in History, perhaps because many of the candidates were alive during the events they were asked to describe. Happily A. J. P. and Max Beloff tied top with 96 per cent.

Everyone failed Maths disgracefully. Godfrey came top with 45 per cent. 'If x is ten,' wrote Frank, in answer to one question, 'does that make me an existentialist?' He got no marks. A. J. P. came second bottom, obviously penalized for being cheeky, and peppering the paper with remarks like 'incomprehensible', 'God knows', and 'What is this?'.

French was also hilarious. The last question asked examinees what they wanted for their birthday. Ludo was penalized for greed for asking for an enormous cake, as was I for demanding twelve bottles of champagne. Godfrey, on the other hand, only asked for one bottle and got two marks. Frank Muir wrote '*Je veux Raquel Welch,*' to which the examiner had added: '*Un peu trop long dans des dents pour vous, mon petit.*'

Frank came top in Geography; A. J. P. who'd got even cheekier came bottom. 'It is a scandal,' he wrote in answer to one question, 'that English landscape should be measured in kilometres.' For a source of energy, he suggested cabinet ministers harnessed to a treadmill for eight hours a day. In answer to questions 5 – 7, he simply wrote: 'To hell with the third world.'

Godfrey came top in English. All the papers were marked now except Joanna Lumley's. Not actually visualizing her as a top academic heavyweight, I averaged out the candidates. Godfrey came top over the six papers with 74 per cent. When I rang to congratulate him, he gave his great ear-splitting bellow of laughter: 'Oh dear, I hope the others won't de-bag me for being a swot.'

Next day, however, Joanna's papers were mailed down to St Peter's, Seaford. Suddenly the competition took on a Eurovision Song Contest excitement, as the Farebrothers marked them, ringing me up through the night, with each result more staggering than the last. She was top in Scripture with 92 per cent, third in History only two points below Beloff and A. J. P., second in Maths, second in French, and finally tied with Godfrey in English, coming out with an incredible average of 82 per cent. What a triumph for the women's movement.

Merci St Peter's, Come in Westminster, where Dr John Rae, the Head Master, had been going through the marked papers, deciding which of the candidates to take. Westminster has a very high C.E. pass mark of 65 per cent.

'I'll take candidate nine at any price,' he said. 'Who is it?'

'Joanna Lumley,' I said.

'My goodness,' gasped Dr Rae. 'She can have a place at Westminster at any time.'

Brian Inglis, Max Beloff, Godfrey and Ludo had also passed and were assured of places. Frank had just failed by *un point*, probably because he'd sent up so many of the papers, but with marks like that he'd have no difficulty getting into a very good school.

Sue Stranks and I alas had both failed. But it was nice that both Dr Rae, and Mike Farebrother in his general summing up, commented on Sue's brilliant talent for improvisation which would no doubt lead to a successful

career in politics. Perhaps she should become the much
needed leader of the SDP.

The final irony was that A. J. P. failed C.E., but Dr Rae
waived the rules and gave him a scholarship to Westminster on the brilliance of his history paper. I hope he doesn't
reduce all the masters to pulp, I would have thought Dr
Rae might have been wiser to recommend A. J. P. to a
special school for gifted pupils.

Here are Dr Rae's comments:

Muir: 64 per cent. Fail. Plausible and unconvincing
candidate despite an occasional touch of humour.
Pin-up mentality on sex and rather a low moral tone
throughout. Would do better at a country boarding
school.
Kennedy: 70 per cent. Pass. Good all-rounder: safe
rather than exciting. There is perhaps rather an un-
healthy knowledge of the Old Testament. But well
worth taking on.
Taylor: 60 per cent. Fail. But awarded scholarship on
'outstanding single subject' principle. Best History
paper I have ever seen. In general rather arrogant and
opinionated though one answer in the Maths paper —
'God knows' — suggests an endearing naïvety. Will
certainly need watching. Place with resilient house-
master.
Beloff: 67 per cent. Pass. Another outstanding History
paper. Irreverent attitude to Scripture suggests inde-
pendence of mind. Dotheboys Hall is his first choice, I
see, but we will take him.
Smith: 74 per cent. Pass. Very able candidate; only

one to make sense of the Maths paper. Rather too well informed about psychiatry for a boy of his age.

Inglis: 66 per cent. Pass – just. Typical product of a certain type of English education: great verbal facility combined with numerical incompetence of striking dimensions.

Stranks: 45 per cent. Fail. On the face of it very weak though with some interesting talents. Makes a little knowledge go a very long way (future politician?) and shows considerable ingenuity in scoring 4 per cent in Maths. Will probably make a million and contribute to some other school's appeal.

Cooper: 58 per cent. Fail. Worthy but lacking in sparkle.

Lumley: 82 per cent. Pass. I like the look of this candidate: thorough, efficient, not spoonfed but equally not falling over backwards to be clever. Just the sort to benefit from education in a good boys' school.

Yally Hoojah

During my first miserable term at boarding school, I heard *Messiah* in Salisbury Cathedral. William Herbert, smiling and sleekly handsome, sang tenor. As 'Comfort Ye, Comfort Ye' echoed softly round the shadowy grey walls, he seemed to be singing directly at me. Basking in the beauty and joy of the music, I forgot my homesickness for a few hours. Afterwards, trying to hide how moved I was, I commented arrogantly to my house mistress that the singing was pretty good for Southerners.

Coming from the West Riding, home of the great choral societies, we did have a slightly proprietorial attitude towards *Messiah*. My husband singing the bass solo at school remembers being sharply put down for questioning the tempo of 'The Trumpet Shall Sound'. 'Just because you live near Huddersfield,' snapped the Precentor, 'it doesn't mean you own the thing.'

Perhaps it's the desire to do justice to a work of such magnitude which causes so much bad temper during rehearsals. My father-in-law used to conduct *Messiah* in the Dales church where he was organist. Unfortunately he didn't get on with the vicar, and frequently started up the organ when he felt the sermon had gone on too long.

This obviously rankled because one year, when he was taking a full dress rehearsal of *Messiah* with chorus and orchestra belting out 'Oonto Oos' (as it's known up there), suddenly the vicar and five minions entered the church bearing a vast Christmas tree. Holding it like a battering ram, they proceeded to march slap through the orchestra, knocking all the music from the stands, and grinding 'Oonto Oos' to a halt.

Whereupon my father-in-law, losing his temper, shouted: 'Take that bloody thing away.'

Whereupon the vicar and his five minions swung round and solemnly carried the tree out again, once more removing every piece of music and the stands as they remarked their footsteps. The vicar reported my father-in-law to the then Bishop of Bradford (a Dr Coggan) who gave him a holy book and ordered him to behave in a more Christian manner in future.

True to the family tradition, this November the house suddenly started to reverberate with bathroom howls of 'Yally Hoojah.'

'We're doing a *Messiah* at Christmas,' announced my daughter. 'On the night there are going to be two trumpets and a drum and real fathers in the choir.' She was furious because she was singing in the altos, who were much naughtier because they were mostly boys, silly twits. No one has more contempt for the opposite sex than a nine-year-old girl.

As the weeks passed she cheered up, and we were regaled with tales of how Daniel had convulsed the altos by bouncing on a whoopee-cushion during 'Glory to God,' and how the little girl sopranos jumped screaming on to their chairs when Andrew dropped a bouncy ball in church and claimed it was a rat, and how the music mistress got simply furious.

The music mistress is in excellent company. Handel used to swear in four languages at anyone – including Royalty who talked during rehearsals. Once he was so infuriated with Carestini, a capricious alto castrato, he threatened to throw him out of the window.

A choir of children in their last years at primary school are probably as hard to keep under control as any eighteenth-century prima donna. Like trying to put a single fitted sheet on a double mattress, you're just forcing the fourth corner in, when the other three leap out.

As I arrived for a rehearsal at the school church last

Friday, the dark dynamic music mistress was trying hard to keep the upper handel.

Smothered in grey duffle coats and holly-berry-red jerseys, the boys with their Rowan Atkinson haircuts, the girls with their flying ponytails, all looked as angelic as any heavenly host. Despite the icy cold of the church and the earliness of the hour, the sopranos were having no difficulty hitting top A, as they romped through 'The Glory of the Lord'. Hanging below her green coat, the orange belt of the music mistress's cardigan twitched like the tail of a marmalade cat with the vigour of her conducting.

'It sounds terrific when you're confident,' she said, calling a halt. 'But do all smile, when I smile at you. And you', she added, turning to the sopranos, 'need more animation.'

Immediately the naughty altos started playing up, mouthing at the sopranos, digging each other in the ribs, and clenching their fists in black-power salutes. Now we moved on to 'Unto Us a Child is Born', everyone going scarlet in the face as they tried to keep 'born' going through fifty-six semi-quavers without drawing breath. 'And the Government shall be upon his shoulder' rang out gloriously on the arctic uncentrally-heated air. Alas an 'everlasting' was screwed up by an adorable blonde in a white headband, who missed top G with an almighty screech, reducing all her row to hysterical giggles.

Suffering from pre-teenage surfeit of energy, all the children kept changing in and out of their duffle coats, readjusting scarves, and putting hoods up and down like sports cars in April. Chair legs of the smallest girls in the front row kept falling down the soi-disant central heating grill, depositing them in the unaccommodating laps of the boys in the row behind.

'Usually we take "Unto Us" a bit quicker,' shouted the music mistress, clicking a faster tempo to the organist.

Instantly the naughty boy altos started clicking their fingers and waggling their hips like pop singers.

'That's enough,' snapped the music mistress. 'Why d'you keep looking at your feet, Richard?'

'Because they're about to drop off,' muttered his next-door neighbour.

Certainly it was getting colder. Breath rose whitely, noses now matched the berry-red jerseys. How unbeautiful are the feet with chilblains.

From a nearby window, a stained-glass St Patrick looked down wide-browed and benign in his mitre. Three snakes squirmed evilly beneath his Billings & Edmonds' house-shoes. His presence seemed appropriate, bearing in mind that the first performance of *Messiah* took place in Dublin, and was such a sell-out that the men in the audience left off their swords, and the women their hoops, so that more people might crowd into the hall. The audience and the press were not only ravished by the music but by Handel's colossal generosity in donating the whole £400 proceeds to charity, which enabled 142 prisoners to be freed from the local debtors' prisons.

I was brought back to earth by the almost unbearable purity of 'There were shepherds abiding in the fields'. Much of the magic of *Messiah* is due to the resonant beauty and simplicity of Jennens's libretto. At least the several recent 'translators' of the Bible have not yet been allowed to substitute their own frightful versions. Or the unfortunate sopranos would find themselves having to cram in: 'There were shepherds in that part of the country/who were spending the night in the fields.' Even worse, the tenor soloist would be forced to sing: 'Every valley shall be filled in.' (Sponsored no doubt by the NCB.)

Or how about the horrors of 'A young woman will become pregnant', for 'Behold! a virgin shall conceive'. My least favourite, however, is 'Listen to this secret truth', replacing the soft enchantments of 'Behold! I tell you a mystery'.

But not content with sabotaging the language of the Bible, the scholars seem hell bent on stripping Handel of every lovely legend which surrounds him. No longer is he allowed to have composed *Messiah* in the grip of divine inspiration, not eating or sleeping for twenty-three days, and seeing God on his throne surrounded by angels. According to scholars now, *Messiah* was written in response to a commission from Dublin, and finished at the double because Handel wanted to get on with *Samson*, his next oratorio. Soon they'll be claiming George II only stood up in the 'Hallelujah Chorus' because he wanted to go to the loo.

Now it was time to Yally Hoojah itself – and a good shout which warmed and cheered everyone up. One soprano went into such a trance while singing that she mindlessly undid and did up one of her plaits. Behind her, two less dedicated angels were eating sweets and surreptitiously mimicking the music mistress, even to the swooping Lord Kitchener points, when she wanted to bring anyone in. Soon the entire row was heaving with supressed mirth and, concentration blown, the final 'King of Kings' came out in a parrot squawk.

Fortunately for them, the music mistress's wrath was instantly diverted by the naughty boy altos who were passing notes and indulging in a spot of Handel jiving.

'We must have a serious attitude to our work,' she shouted, ginger tail quivering. 'If you fool around it puts me off, and everything's spoilt.'

'I've got an earache,' moaned a little brunette.

With superhuman effort, tempers were restored, and the music mistress gave the child her scarf.

'Now we've got five minutes left, let's go back to our favourite difficult bit: "Unto Us".'

Everyone groaned, the sopranos did highkicks to keep warm. Like a woman's four at the tennis club desperately keeping a rally going, the choir struggled to the final 'Prince of Peace'.

'Thank you very much,' said the music mistress. 'Carry your chairs back to the hall, and remember no hands in pockets and no talking or fidgeting on the night.'

And none of them did. Like true primary donnas they all rose to the occasion. Holding their own splendidly against the drum, and the silver snarling trumpets, and the real fathers singing tenor and bass. As Handel replied when congratulated on the first English performance of *Messiah*:

'I should be sorry if I just entertained people. I wanted to make them better.' And he did that.

School crawl

At the risk of sounding more sexist than usual, I've never lost much sleep over my daughter's education. She was always blissfully happy at her primary school, her reports were respectable, I simply assumed that this autumn when she was eleven she would move on to one of the local secondary schools.

The only problem was that our part of Putney is a Humbert Humbert's paradise, swarming with little girls of Emily's age – all nice children basically – but endlessly squabbling. Last summer the dissension spread to the mothers and became so venomous that I decided to opt out of the whole day-school rat race, and send her instead to a boarding school. I was egged on, I may add, by Emily herself who'd just read all the *Malory Towers* books, and was mad for midnight feasts and glory on the lacrosse field.

Having heard that Tudor Hall was a very happy school, I wrote in June to the headmistress, who wrote back saying that they were booked solid until autumn 1983 but would I like to come down to Banbury for a chat? As Emily had to leave her current school by summer 1982 and couldn't exactly walk the streets for a year, this seemed pointless.

I then fired off letters to five other schools and was slightly alarmed to be told that they were all so booked up interviewing parents that they couldn't see me until October.

Having been a disaster at school myself, I am absolutely terrified by headmistresses. In October, wearing a tweed coat and skirt in a vain attempt to look sensible and conservative, I set off on a school crawl. My husband, who still adopts the attitude that One Can get One's Child into Any School One Wants, informed me he was not going to have any part in 'all this sucking up'. He did, however, offer to drive me down to the first school, which was in Berkshire, but insisted on staying in the car to edit a manuscript on the Gurkhas.

Both Emily and I were absolutely enchanted by the school. Despite the very high academic standards, the girls all looked happy and relaxed. The grounds were beautiful, with lots of amiable dogs wandering about, and there was a cosy junior house to soften the blow of leaving home. What impressed me most, however, was that the young and attractive headmistress, although charming to me, was far more interested in talking to Emily and finding out what she thought about life. The only discordant note was when a nice house mistress took us back to the car park, and Leo, having been dragged reluctantly out to be introduced, said he felt editing the Gurkhas must take precedence over Emily's school career. Felt strongly that he would not qualify as a sufficiently 'caring and concerned' parent.

On to one of my old schools in the West Country – minus Leo. We arrived hours early, but went in almost immediately because the set of parents before us had failed to show up. 'Shall we leave "Emma" in the waiting room while we have a chat,' said the attractive and even younger headmistress. Emily, left with mildewed copies of *Punch*, looked bootfaced.

As usual during interviews, I could think of no searching questions to ask about the school. Much of the time was, therefore, taken up with the headmistress telling me she was worried because they only had just over 270 girls in the school, and the governors wanted her to up the numbers to 300. Felt this was a refreshing change from all the people who claim their schools are booked up to the year 2000.

Finally Emily was summoned. 'Well Emma,' said the headmistress warmly, 'the most important thing is that

108

you really want to come here.' Emily smiled back with passionate insincerity.

Discipline, which was positively Draconian in my day, had obviously been relaxed. We were shown round by a beautiful prefect wearing a great deal of purple eye-shadow. A kind house mistress gave me the only cup of tea I was offered during my school crawl.

We were also impressed by Wycombe Abbey, where we were interviewed by yet another tremendously attractive headmistress, whose long beautiful legs made me glad I'd abandoned my sensible skirt and reverted to trousers. Like all schools with high academic standards, she was at pains to point out that Wycombe was not an intellectual sweat-shop. The only girls who didn't really fit in, she went on, were the dreamy ones. Alas, that was the death knell. Emily, who has her head in the clouds even more than her mother, wouldn't stand a chance.

To get into boarding school, you have to take a Common Entrance exam. Boys take this at thirteen, girls from ten onwards. When I saw a copy of last year's paper for girls, which in its own way was as tough as the boys' C.E. exam we had all taken the year before, I nearly fainted. For the first time I realized what Emily was up against. English Comprehension was a stinker and neither of us could finish the Maths paper. Felt lacerated with remorse and panic that – unlike almost every other mother in Putney – I hadn't had her coached years ago. Went straight home and hired Maths and English tutors.

As you can only take Common Entrance for one school, we settled for the first school we saw in Berkshire. But what if she didn't get in? Decided to enter her for some of the London schools. As they don't use C.E., you can try as many as you like. Most children in Emily's class were taking exams for six or seven different schools.

November and December seemed to be entirely occupied with registering Emily for Putney High School, More House in Pont Street, and St Paul's, and spending a bomb on registration and exam fees. 'But you do realize London schools are far more difficult to get into than boarding schools?' asked a local harpy scathingly.

January: The pressure was really on. All anyone could talk about was education. Fathers glazed at drinks parties and mothers gathered in huddles in the street could be seen tearing their hair. Noticed that mothers without jobs tended to be far more pushy and uptight, because they had nothing to think about except driving their children on to double firsts with a bayonet and a pitchfork.

In an attempt to wean Emily off Enid Blyton, we read Oscar Wilde, Kipling, Arthur Ransome, and even Tennyson together. English coaching was coming on well. Unfortunately the Maths tutor had to come from Sunbury-on-Thames and missed several weeks because of Christmas and snow-bound roads. Like Napoleon, we were battling with Generals Janvier and Février.

Endless time was also spent perjuring myself on various application forms. *Which is your first choice of school?* was one of the knottier questions. 'Always put down the school to which you're applying,' said a friend airily, 'and mention only one other. Then pray like hell the schools don't confer.'

Is your daughter being coached? was another. At least I didn't go as far as one Protestant friend, who, when applying for an RC school, wrote down that she was an ardent Catholic.

St Paul's wanted Emily's birth certificate and a photograph. Other schools wanted references. Put down Godfrey Smith, Emily's godfather, who is the only person I know of sufficient consequence, and made mental note to make acquaintance of some bishops.

Towards the end of January, a week before Emily started the exams, hysteria was rising:

'What did you do today, darling?'

'Oh, mucked about.'

'Didn't you do any practice papers?'

'No – we're doing a project on snakes.'

110

'Jesus! And no homework?'

Emily then pointed out with perfect logic, that as almost the entire form were away from school already taking exams for Wimbledon High, Lady Eleanor Holles and Godolphin and Latymer, it wasn't fair to give homework to the handful of children left.

Horrific stories were filtering through about the difficulty of the Godolphin and Latymer exam, which coincided with a day when the trains struck. Several mothers, not realizing how the traffic snarled up in the rush hour, arrived late for the exam. Others stormed the bus lanes like Valkyries.

'There were literally hundreds of children competing for a handful of places,' said one discouraged mother. 'They all came out as white as sheets, poor lambs.'

On 30 January Emily took her first exam, at More House. She was so excited, you'd have thought she was going to a disco. Dressed in tight crimson cords, blue ankle boots, and a pink jersey embroidered with flowers, she clutched her new pencil box, and like Squirrel Nutkin danced up and down like a sunbeam. Two of her best friends from another school who were taking the same exam arrived to collect us. Both children were quite unrecognizable wearing coats and shirts, tights and strap shoes, and with their hair scraped back into perfect plaits.

'Oh Emily,' said one in horror, 'our form mistress said we'd never pass an exam in trousers.'

One of the children's mothers gave us a lift to More House. 'I spent last night with a sample paper,' she said, 'giving Rosamund a crash course in parts of speech.'

Emily came out of the exam in raging high spirits. 'Easy peasy,' she crowed. 'I couldn't do the Maths, but we had those things you taught me in the car. An adverb does describe a noun doesn't it?' Oh hubris, hubris.

Next it was Putney High School. I rose at dawn with a punishing hangover. As we drove through the deserted streets of Putney, suddenly we started seeing little girls, deathly pale, as though they'd spent their entire lives down the mines, converging on the school. Some were accompanied by tieless bug-eyed fathers, others by twitching chain-smoking mothers. Housewives red in tooth and claw. Many were tugged along by the regulation Battersea mongrel, recently acquired to 'relate to' the child over this stressful time. You could feel the white-hot hiss of competition; it was like the final judging at Crufts.

I checked Emily in with my mouth tightly shut, so the mistress behind the desk wouldn't be asphyxiated by last night's brandy fumes. Then was nearly knocked sideways by local mother storming past, having blazing row with screaming child.

One unbelievable mother (whose child at Putney High's junior school had not only been assured a place at the senior school, but had also got over 80 per cent in all her mock exams) had actually pulled the child out of school the day before the exam and had her coached from nine in the morning until nine at night. Ray Buckton would never stand for that.

Emily came home from the exam less euphoric. The Maths once again had been the stumbling block.

Two exams down – and two to go. To add to the complications, the following Tuesday Emily was summoned to interviews at More House and St Paul's within three-quarters of an hour of one another. Toyed with the idea of hiring a helicopter. Instead telephoned St Paul's, and lied that I had to interview a cabinet minister that morning, and could they change the time of interview. St Paul's replied with commendable intransigence that I would have to change the cabinet minister.

Unnerved by fellow mother who told me she'd been giving her child comprehension tests every night for the past six weeks and also conducting mock interviews. 'Interviews are very important,' she went on. One child had evidently got a scholarship when, on being shown a picture postcard, she had identified it as a Turner.

Peeling onions that night I attempted to interview Emily:

ME: Give me the names of some famous painters.

EMILY (*after long pause*): Wasn't there one called Monica Lisa?

ME: Who lives at No. 10?

EMILY: Mrs Thatcher.

ME: And at No. 11?

EMILY: Mr Thatcher.

ME: Who are your favourite writers?

EMILY: Oscar Wilde and Enid Blyton.

Spent several minutes explaining why given the prejudices of today's educationalists, Rudyard Kipling was a more suitable choice than Enid Blyton.

Another headache was what she should wear for these interviews. School uniform, groaning with every badge you can borrow, advised a friend. Unfortunately, Emily's school dresses, because it's her last year and I am too mean to fork out for new ones, were welded together with safety-pins, and just covered her groin. We plumped for a grey jersey and a red midi. On the morning of the interview we disastrously found the red midi covered in marks and curled up under Emily's bed like a hedgehog. Had to opt for rust mini with small slit at front.

We arrived at More House ridiculously early in the hope of getting away early, leaving the minicab waiting outside, ready to race us across London to St Paul's.

'What questions did she ask you?' demanded a twitching mother, as brilliant-looking child wearing uniform weighed down with badges, came out of the headmistress's room. Nearly fell off my chair trying to catch brilliant child's answer.

'Remember to say *Life on Earth* and not *Dallas* is your favourite programme,' urged another twitching mother, as the next child went in.

Next moment disaster struck again as Emily leapt up to look at a picture – and, as a result of ten million packets of crisps consumed over the last ten years, split her skirt up the front. Too late to ask for a needle and cotton, but just time to turn the skirt round back to front, before she was summoned.

She came out very bullish, having adored the headmistress. 'I said *The Happy Prince* was my favourite story, and when she asked me what schools I was trying for, I remembered every one!'

And I'd only admitted to one other school on her form.

So thrown was I by this piece of information, that it was only as we shot round Hyde Park Corner that I realized the minicab was belting us towards St Paul's Cathedral, not School. By a frantic U-turn and Formula 1 driving, we reached the school on time. Emily was promptly whisked in to see the educational psychiatrist. At least on the couch he wouldn't see her split skirt.

I joined the other mothers waiting in the hall. Green-eyed monsters armed with pitchforks and bayonets with *The Guardian* unread on their knees, and steam coming out of their ears. I was beginning to recognize many of them from Putney High and More House. It was like some ghastly musical chairs, with all of us stalking each other round the schools, knowing there weren't going to be enough places left at the end.

'If Susan gets into St Paul's,' said one mother, 'we'll move house from Maidenhead to London.'

A woman in coloured stockings gazed at me beadily: 'Are you trying for an organ award?'

I shook my head.

'What does your daughter play?'

'Nothing.'

They all looked at me in horror. I then noticed all the little girls were clutching sheet music to their bosoms, and realized I'd fallen among the music scholarship candidates.

All the mothers were in a frightful tizz because some vile, extra bright child was turning up that afternoon who was going to play the Bach Piano Sonata. 'That's at least Grade 8,' hissed the woman in fawn. 'She's sure to walk it.'

The woman in coloured stockings now turned her beady eyes on a small child holding a book of Scarlatti sonatinas. 'You've brought your music have you? My daughter always plays without her music, it gives a better impression.' Mercifully she was then distracted by another child who came out carrying a cello.

'How did you get on, darling?' screamed her mother.

'Oh they played a tune on the piano, and I played it straightaway on my cello.'

All around, you could hear the gnashing of capped teeth.

Emily came out from the psychiatrist and went in to see the Deputy High Mistress. The smell of school lunch drifted down the passage, St Paul's incumbents shuffled past, their punk hair-styles rising like cockscombs. Emily seemed to have been in with the deputy head for ages.

'Oh they always keep the borderline cases in longest,' said a woman in crimson crushingly.

'Who's the educational psychiatrist?' I asked.

'Some boffin,' said the woman in fawn, 'who's heavily into the middle classes and gifted children. If you have an IQ over 170, you're known as severely gifted.'

This alas was not to be Emily's problem. She came out grinning broadly. 'I got in a muddle and said my favourite writer was Oscar Blyton.'

Thursday: Gruelling day Putney High interview first thing in the morning. In the afternoon, Emily had to take her first St Paul's exam and I had to take the dogs to Crufts to be interviewed by Russell Harty as the first mongrels ever to break through the breed-dog barrier. I had reached that bombed state when I was solemnly plaiting the junior dog's whiskers, and forcing a dog car-sick pill, buried in a piece of cheese, down Emily.

Worried about traffic, Emily and I arrived at Putney High hours early and watched more nubile girls with cockscomb hair walking up and down.

'Can I have punk hair if I get into Putney High?'

'Anything, anything.'

I had a brief interview with the headmistress, who's a darling, kind and wise with a great sense of humour. She asked me if I'd got anything to tell her about Emily. Resisted temptation to lay head on desk, burst into tears, and plead with her to give Emily a place.

Emily went in after me, and emerged very crestfallen. She'd got in a muddle over *The Jungle Book* and *Just So Stories*, and had forgotten Baloo's name. She suddenly looked very tired, and her high spirits were beginning to flag.

On to St Paul's, who very sensibly have the children in for two whole half days to see how they bear up both in exams and lessons. I rang up Emily from Crufts to see how she'd got on.

'Oh we had a really fun time dissecting maggots, and the man who took us was ginormous, seven foot at least. Oh, the exam, I couldn't do that at all.'

Impossible not to plunge into the blackest of glooms. Bed after Russell Harty at two o'clock.

Friday: Up at 6.45, panicking about getting to St Paul's during the train strike. Arrived an hour early to find plenty of mothers milling about, all looking absolutely knackered.

Went home and, for the umpteenth day running, failed to work. At this rate, even if by some miracle Emily did get in somewhere, we'd never be able to pay the fees. Clutching at straws, looking for a sign, I read Emily's horoscope and then mine – both frightful.

Back at St Paul's at 2.30 to pick Emily up. By now the green-eyed monsters were getting seriously on each other's nerves.

'My daughter's a very well developed young lady,' announced a fat woman. 'I hope they don't think she's much older than she is.'

'Should have given her a face lift beforehand,' muttered a woman in knickerbockers savagely.

'My daughter's at a state school,' went on the fat woman. 'I've put so much work into the PTA and the Board of Governors and the school play I haven't had a moment to myself for five years. I said to Harold: this time round we're going to pay.'

'State-school children don't stand a chance,' said another mother in a loud whisper. 'They aren't sufficiently programmed.'

'I've worked so hard on my child, I'll die if she doesn't get in,' sighed a woman in a folk-weave skirt. 'Mind you, she found yesterday's exam so easy she finished it half an hour early.'

'Over confident – bad sign,' muttered the woman in knickerbockers, swallowing a Valium.

Here we go round the prickly parent.

Next they moved on to how exhausted they were all feeling. Some had rashes, others cystitis, others migraines.

'No wonder they abolished the eleven plus,' said a pretty woman in a mink waistcoat. 'The working classes could never have coped with this kind of strain.'

'I'm so run down,' said a grey-haired mother, scratching frantically, 'I've got scalp eczema all over my head.'

On either side, mothers edged away.

The hall was now packed with frantically apprehensive parents, including several sheepish-looking fathers. Why do men always look like eunuchs when they're heavily outnumbered by women? None of this lot would have qualified for the organ award.

Suddenly children started swarming out, being hysterically interrogated.

'Hallelujah! last exam,' said a blinking father.

Next minute his daughter had rushed up like Lizzie Borden and was whacking him over the head with her pencil box.

Emily drifted out with the usual stream of cocktail party chat.

117

'Really fun again, fish and chips for lunch, and in one room there's a skeleton called Charlie and a bare man made of clay with a willie.'

'How did the exam go?'

'Awful, I couldn't do the last two pages at all. Why are you looking so sad Mummy?'

The weekend was traumatic. All Emily could think about was buying some pink hair spray for a punk party on Saturday and getting into the netball team. I panicked and felt I ought to give her some last-minute coaching before her Monday's exam for the boarding school in Berkshire. Two hours were spent on Sunday afternoon going through last year's Maths C.E. paper and trying not to lose our tempers.

As I tucked her up that night, she suddenly asked in a small voice what would happen if she didn't get in anywhere. Downstairs Leo accused me of over-reacting hysterically and transmitting my fear to Emily, which triggered off a full-dress row in which I accused him of never taking any interest in his children's education, and not even bothering to wish Emily good luck before her exams.

Monday: After a sleepless night, lay in bed contemplating suicide. Downstairs I heard Leo loudly saying good luck to each dog and cat, then good luck to Emily and finally good luck to each of the goldfish. Hastily decided against suicide.

Emily went off to her Common Entrance. Unable to concentrate, I took the dogs for a long cold walk. Ludicrously cast down, when one magpie for sorrow rose raucously out of a hawthorn bush. Then suddenly a kingfisher flashed downstream, a thing of such blue incandescent beauty with its coral belly aflame that it must be a good omen. Oh please God, let her always be as free and happy and fulfilled.

Emily returned in good spirits. The English had been nice, and the Maths not so awful as she'd expected.

'I'm now going to spend the rest of the year learning to knit, cook and play rounders.'

Nothing really returned to normal for the next month until the results came out. I just bit my nails, and watched the post, and had long gloomy discussions with other mothers as to whether we ought to start looking at other schools.

'Oh, I expect Emily'll scrape in somewhere,' said one charmer. 'You are a name, and they might bend the rules to have someone to open their fêtes.'

Then one Saturday morning early in March, at the first moment when I wasn't worrying myself sick, a letter arrived from the school in Berkshire offering Emily a place. Promptly burst into tears of joy and hugged her until her ribs cracked. Understood exactly how our own Godfrey Smith (when one of his daughters was offered a place at a London day school) promptly sent the first term's fees round in a taxi before they had time to change their minds. Ecstatically rang up school in Berkshire and accepted. Farewell the tranquillized mind.

On 12 March, the London results came through. As expected Emily had ploughed St Paul's, but got into More House and Putney High.

'I always knew she'd do it,' said Leo. 'If you hadn't hassled her she'd have probably got a place at St Paul's.'

As Queen Victoria once wrote to the Princess Royal: 'Education can be overdone.'

Further scenes
of revelry

Charitably having a ball

Any invitation I get to a charity ball goes straight into the dustbin. Maybe I lack public spirit, but I refuse to be bullied by some double-barrelled gorgon who hasn't enough to do in the afternoon into squandering a fortune on tickets in order to join a pack of social climbers at a party where there's no hostess, and one is expected to pay four times as much for drink as one does at home.

Admittedly when I was unattached I rather enjoyed such occasions, because one sometimes met new men, and because I liked dancing, and used to flail around the floor like a clockwork maenad not giving a stuff how silly I looked. But ever since *Harpers* listed me as one of the worst dancers in London, I'm so overwhelmed with self-consciousness, it needs a fork-lift truck or half a bottle of Gordons to get me on to the floor.

It was not therefore with vast enthusiasm that Leo and I embarked on a ball crawl recently taking in the Wheels Ball and the Golden Eagle Ball on Saturday night, and the Royal Caledonian Ball on the following Monday.

The Wheels Ball, held at Grosvenor House, was given by a rather raffish combination of the Show Business Car Club, and the Motor Traders and Manufacturers Association. The handout promised that 'many famous names from show business and the motor industry would be present.' I had visions of myself rhumba-ing the night away in the arms of Red Robbo, or kicking off my shoes to be on an eye-level with Sir Michael Edwardes.

We arrived to find Grosvenor House crawling with more balls than a Wimbledon final. Having tried the British Safety Council Ball, and the hotel dinner dance, and dancing to Ella Fitzgerald upstairs, we ended up in a room with lots of women in lurex, and men with maroon faces wearing tartan bow ties. It was several minutes before we realized we'd strayed into the London and Provincial Fruit Buyers' Ball by mistake.

When we finally located our ball in the Great Hall, it was deserted except for a white Ford Fiesta up for raffle and some ball-bearing manufacturers with duck-egg-blue frills cascading out of their dinner jackets talking to a lot of women in transparent capes. Next minute, a toastmaster was urging us 'to hurry along to the bar to sample a few jars'. According to the table lists, Dee Dee Wilde, Roy Kinnear and Alvin Stardust would be present. Bacchus had also booked three tables, so it looked as though we were in for a wild evening.

The long gallery was now filling up with men looking hot-eyed and slightly degenerate like characters out of *Dallas*. Their wives exuded that barely repressed lasciviousness that comes from sunbathing naked on the roof all week.

A staggering amount of women were wearing trousers, mostly tight black satin, topped with black sequinned jackets, or with those frightful knee-length shifts – presumably to hide the bulges. Capes were everywhere, reminding one of those plastic contraptions women sometimes tie round their necks while making-up – to protect their clothes from powder and scurf. One girl wore a white dress so fantastically festooned with pink ribbon she must have been gift-wrapped at Harrods.

The change in men's clothes was even more dramatic with dinner jackets rampaging in all colours not in the rainbow: ox-blood, crimson, mauve, kingfisher blue, maroon, even ginger.

'Dinner suits go out of fashion so quickly,' explained a motor mechanic's wife, 'that most men hire them these days.' Sterling Moss Bros, perhaps.

Presumably in the past people plunged into ox-blood or kingfisher blue to avoid the thunderous possibility of being mistaken for a waiter. Alas, the waiters at Grosvenor House have outsmarted them by going into slate-blue dinner jackets with dark-blue lapels, and now look just like customers.

On the way to the tombola, I passed Shaw Taylor, radiating automatic benevolence like a plain clothes Father Christmas. And in fact the tombola laid out on a long table looked not unlike a display of burglars' loot from *Police Five*. For £5 for two tickets, you could win anything from a fridge to a tin of Rover Assorted Biscuits.

People seem to have a touching faith in potential tombola booty. A few years ago, just before an actor friend of mine was leaving for one of the great theatrical charity balls, he had a telephone call telling him his son had won a scholarship to Eton. Highly delighted, he broadcast the good news to everyone he met at the ball – as he was leaving two East End show-business tycoons came and pumped him by the hand, saying: 'What a wonderful thing, Harry, to win a scholarship to Eton on the tombola!'

Tonight a lugubrious individual looked much less amused at winning a garden spade, and stalked off as though he was going to bury his mother. A woman in spotted orange, resembling a very old goldfish crossed with a trout, was equally cast down to be handed some sparking plugs.

One of the organizers told me numbers were badly down this year. 'In times of inflation,' she went on, sounding rather like a vet, 'balls seem to be the first things people cut out.'

Despite this, the Wheels Ball eventually netted an incredible £15,000 for charity. At the bar, a vast amount of expense-account money was changing hands. The aim of the evening seemed to be getting your business card into the breast pockets of as many people as possible.

'It's crucial,' said a motor trader, 'to be seen at these functions.'

As we went down to dinner, show-business people everywhere could be heard saying: 'I'll get my agent to get in touch with your agent.'

Terpsichore Ltd seemed to have merged with Mammon Inc.

Our party joined up with the ball's golden-haired publicity girl, who was only drinking soda water. She'd brought her boyfriend who played the guitar, and a gynaecologist who turned out far more excitingly to be a sexologist. He'd been appointed official doctor to the Show Business Car Club, but as they never seem to have any smashes on their rallies (one member – Adrian Love of Capital Radio – doesn't even drive) he spends his time sexing cars instead. Hondas and BMWs are evidently male, but Alfa-Romeos female. He and I were soon nose to nose over sex drives.

The dinner was awful. But I was so transfixed by a description of how one could cure premature ejaculation in seven months, I hardly touched my smoked mackerel. The guitarist on my left tried to raise the tone by talking about Vivaldi, but was overwhelmed by a manic grinding, not unlike the gears at Silverstone, as all the plates were cleared away. Mackerel was followed by a main course of linoleum in warmed-up Oxo.

'*Parents* magazine,' said the sexologist, chewing away like a football manager at a Cup Final, 'recently commissioned me to write a piece on the clitoris. The subject was so compelling I wrote 2,000 words. Alas, they were savagely cut.' Shades of the Kikuyu.

'What should one do,' said the guitarist, clearing his throat and going pink, 'when someone wants to try something that the other finds revolting, I mean a friend of mine . . .'

'Paedophilia?' asked the sexologist calmly.

Mercifully perhaps *The Sunday Times*'s photographer who had also got lost and had been playing oranges and lemons upstairs at the Fruiterers' Ball, arrived and bore me off to talk to the toastmaster, who had polished silver hair, and looked like Mike Yarwood impersonating Lord Carrington.

'Such a riveting conversation about sex,' I said.

'Tell me,' said the toastmaster. 'I am very broadminded.'

On receiving a précis, he went puce. 'Rather strong for a function of this nature. If you'll excuse me,' he went on, 'I'll just slip away and organize the loyal toast. With people clamouring to smoke, one has it earlier and earlier these days – before the sweet, or as Prince Charles would say the "pud-ding".'

With a whisk of red tails, he disappeared through the curtains.

'He's a bit miffed tonight,' said a banqueting manager. 'Hasn't enough to do. Being show-business folk here tonight, they want to do all the announcing themselves.'

Through the curtains came the drum roll of the National Anthem. 'Even got the Queen on tape,' sniffed a waiter. 'This sort of do won't fork out for a dinner band any more.'

The toastmaster returned and sank heavily into a chair. 'Then there's the mode of dress,' he continued. 'All those coloured dinner suits, men just like peacocks. There's a different class of person attending balls these days. Oh they behave all right, but there's no breedin' about. Take that Alvin Starlight, he looks OK tonight, but he sat next to the Duke of Kent the other night with no tie, and an open neck filled with necklaces.'

His main complaint, however, was that after dinner the band would be playing unceasingly.

'What happens to some poor young man stuck with his boss's wife as a duty dance? How can he return her to the table when there's no break in the music? He could be left dancing with her all night. In the old days, Victor Sylvester played three tunes, then struck a continued chord, so people knew a dance was over. Partners should be changed often like nappies.'

Back in the hall, a tremendous amount of drink was being consumed. Spending so much time underneath cars, one half expected the mechanics to roll over and slide under the table head first.

*   *   *

127

We decided to change balls, moving on to the Golden Eagle Ball at the Savoy, given by that resplendent gynocracy, the American Women's Club in London. At the thought of all those birds of prey awaiting us, we all got slightly frivolous. No doubt the toastmaster would exhort us to hurry along to the bar to sample a few night jars.

In the Savoy Ladies' loo, the din of twanging panti-girdles was not unlike the plates clattering at Grosvenor House, as huge relentlessly jolly Lady Eagles, crying 'Ow', and 'Warll', and 'Oo-oo', upstaged each other about 'stopping arf at Bangkok before going on', applied crimson lipstick, and washed their hands with extreme thoroughness after going to the lavatory.

Descending to the ballroom, we passed a large woman clad almost entirely in swansdown. One of our party started clucking like a hen who's just laid an egg.

My husband and a girl from our party had already gone on ahead to warn the eagles of our arrival, and been met with a very frosty reception. We thought you were not coming, they said. The table had been cleared, so Leo had bought a bottle of whisky at £19 (the water was evidently free). By the time we arrived, the bottle was half empty and he was on the floor, cannoning off large ladies rather like a competitor in a stock car race. The Americans were behaving in a much more circumspect way, he reported, than the motor mechanics, and looked rather cleaner.

A friendly Junoesque blonde in powder blue told me that the Golden Eagles were primarily a social club. Proceeds of the evening, I found out later, amounted to £1,500 and went to Great Ormond Street Hospital. A Mrs Edward Streator had kindly opened her eyrie for a free luncheon, and everyone instead of paying had bought prizes for the tombola.

Over the din of 'Yellow River' — or is it 'Yellow Ribbon' — I tried to talk to the Golden Eagle president, who had swept-up hair and one of those splendid figures that reminded me of the Proust hostess who was advised against starting a salon, because she had too luscious a bosom to keep the conversation general.

'There are three ladies in the receiving line,' yelled the president. 'To begin with there's the vulture.'

I wrote down 'vulture'.

'No,' she yelled, ' "Vollture".'

Thinking this must be American spelling, I wrote down 'Vollture'.

'No,' she yelled, and wrote down 'Ball Chairman'.

'Oh,' I yelled, 'Bawl Chairman.'

We gave up. As David Soul said on television the other night, 'There is a language barrier'.

The programme, which had a splendid gold cover, was filled with advertisements from huge corporations wishing the American Women's Club a Happy and Successful Evening.

Golden eagles, explained one petroleum ad, have been known to frighten wolves by descending on them from a great height. That must be why all the husbands were behaving so well on the dance floor. If their hands wandered they might have got beaked. They also all wore black dinner jackets. Eagles obviously don't like peacocks.

A ball-dozer waltzed up to my husband: 'May I have the pleasure of Mr Jilly Cooper?' she said.

Some sadist in our party then suggested I should be photographed dancing with the archetypally bald American. So *The Sunday Times*'s photographer dragged me on to the floor for a bald crawl searching for likely victims. Eventually he swooped on some engineer from Hampstead Garden Suburb with a polished pate, who looked utterly bemused, but who was too polite to refuse. Decorously we circled, he like Fred Astaire, I, alas, like Gingerly Rogers.

Back at our table, the Lady Eagles still looking determinedly supportive, but I felt that their good manners were being overstrained. One girl in our party kept forgetting Carter's Christian name and referring to him as Old Peanuts. 'I adore American women's beautifully shaved armpits,' said her husband. 'Not at all Muskie,' she added. They both collapsed in giggles.

Not wanting to get beaked for silliness either, I decided we had better return to the motor traders for breakfast.

Back in the crepuscular gloom of Grosvenor House, everyone was dancing with fantastic energy, their arms and legs going like pistons. Most of the men had removed their collars and ties, a spotlight roved around the floor wiping the leers off faces. Breakfast sadly seemed to have been replaced by 'tea and gâteaus'. The sexologist, who'd progressed to bisexuality, suggested a dance. But knowing the alleged correlation between being a bad dancer and being lousy in bed, I offered him a cream tart instead.

For the cabaret, four sisters from Manchester called Jeep sang songs by Glen Miller, then launched into the American Battle Hymn. As the 'Glory Hallelujahs' rang out, one felt they'd got their balls crossed, and ought to be at the Savoy saluting the Lady Eagles. Then Shaw Taylor drew the raffles, and a lot of the prizewinners had extreme difficulty scaling the Eiger-like face of the eighteen-inch stage.

A tall man came up and shook my hand:

'May I salute a fellow columnist,' he cried, 'I am Diogenes from *What's On*. It is indeed hard to write up a function like this without ruffling show-business feathers.'

The handsomest man in the room was dancing round in a purple and green striped skirt with a comely blonde who was wearing his dinner jacket and hanging on to his braces. Last time I'd met him, he'd spent half an hour trying to sell a BMW to some Arab – Car-floggi, perhaps.

Next minute he was leading a vast conga which came thundering towards us. He got very cross when my husband rose up like a traffic cop and diverted them in the wrong direction, they were half way to the kitchens before they realized their mistake.

130

Finally everyone sang 'Land of Hope and Glory', crowding round the band, and waving invisible scarves from side to side, like windscreen wipers in a traffic jam. A trick presumably picked up from watching too much *Match of the Day*.

'I told you there was no breeding about any more,' said the toastmaster sadly, as he set out for home.

He would probably have been much happier at the Royal Caledonian Ball on Monday, which after the *arriviste* thrusting of the motor traders, and the middle-class decorum of the Lady Eagles, was distinctly more patrician in flavour.

It was only on the Sunday before, when my husband looked at the tickets, that he saw he was expected to wear a white tie. 'Persons wearing dinner jackets will not be admitted,' said the ticket sternly. So it was off to Moss Bros for him, no doubt meeting the motor traders on the return journey.

I hadn't a smarter dress to wear either, so I decided to change the colour of my skin with tan out of a bottle. The effect was rather dramatic – except for brilliant orange elbows, and hands that looked as though I'd been reading an orange book too long in the bath.

Tickets that night didn't include dinner, which meant that, by eight o'clock, the lilac- and laburnum-lined streets of Chelsea and Belgravia were swarming with young men in kilts carrying bottles, accompanying little girls in white dresses topped by tartan sashes to pre-ball dinner parties. It was the ideal night for a ball. A warm breeze caressed bare arms, and hairy knees, and Hyde Park seemed to tremble with emergent greenness and promise.

Inside the Grosvenor House ballroom, Peter Townend, social editor of *The Tatler*, was purring away like a well-oiled Bentley. No, he hadn't bothered to attend the Wheels Ball or the Golden Eagle Ball, he said dismissively, any ball held in London on Saturday was socially not on.

Certainly, running an eye over the table lists which

included Princess Margaret, the Duke of Atholl, the Moncreiffe of that Ilk, and the Master of Colville, it looked as though we were in for an infinitely smarter evening. In fact it was like stepping back eighty years in time.

Instead of the twilit gloom of the motor mechanics' ball, the Great Hall blazed with lights. Pretty girls, their faces accentuated by excitement rather than make-up, wore flowing, waisted dresses straight out of Ingres or Alma-Tadema, and their hair piled up and garlanded with flowers and jewels. They were filling in dance programmes in round schoolgirl handwriting:

> *Dashing White Sergeant:* Nick.
> *Eightsome Reel:* Johnnie.
> *Fox-Trot:* Henry?

Their mothers were magnificent too, with their rounded magnolia-white shoulders, Scotch mist soft complexions, and glittering diamonds and pearls. Even well into their fifties, their unwrinkled, untroubled beauty had no need of dimmer light.

The men were even more breathtaking. One could see exactly why Lydia Bennet and her sister got so intoxicated by all those red coats of the Blankshire Regiment. There were also some devastating older men in tails with silk scarlet facings. Others wore kilts and velvet doublets in dark blues and greens with silver belts and buckles, and white lace cascading from their sleeves and throats. It was as though hundreds of Young Lochinvars had come out of the West End. They were even more peacocky than the motor traders, but distinguished by complete self-assurance, and the fact that a pleated skirt looks so well on lean patrician hips and flat stomachs. There should have been a Belly of the Ball contest.

Pipers from the Duke of Atholl's private army opened the ball with a splendid din. Then came Princess Margaret led by the towering Duke of Atholl, followed by seventeen sets of the best dancers to give us some demonstration reels.

Princess Margaret looking brown and pretty, in a white dress held up by diamante straps, danced very well. You couldn't see her feet as she moved, it was as thought she were gliding around on casters. Speculation as to the nature of her recent operation proved utterly fruitless too, because with their totally dead-pan expressions, everyone on the floor looked as though their faces had been lifted anyway. Occasionally the men gave strange unearthly wails like trains going into a tunnel.

The Duke of Atholl scuttled round like Mrs Tittle-mouse. 'I was at prep school with him,' said my husband. 'In those days he was called Murray, G. I. There was another boy called Murray there at the same time who once ate a worm for a bet outside Gargrave.'

Demonstration reels over, everyone else poured on to the floor for the Dashing White Sergeant (who must have been the only man without a commission in the room) saying 'Har you, Alastair?' 'Har you, Caroline?' to each other.

'Leggings, har you?' everyone screamed, falling on a plump youth with a pink face and a braying laugh.

'You should have got here earlier, Alastair,' said pink and white blonde, smugly consulting her programme. 'I *simply* haven't got room to fit you in.'

At the other end of the scale, a poor little girl with spectacles concealed a totally empty programme behind her back, as one hides one's empty glass in a pub.

Our party, all English, were put at a table with a group of officers from the Duke's private army and their wives. They were all very polite, but at first treated us with that slight wariness that David Attenborough displayed on television recently when he was cuddling up to a family of gorillas in the wild. Tribally across the table were laid point-to-handle all their knives – the skean-dhus, which Scotsmen keep in their socks.

A moment later I was tempted to plunge one into the

133

secretary of the ball, who trundled up in a towering rage saying *The Sunday Times*'s photographer couldn't come in because he was improperly dressed in a dark suit, and what would Princess Margaret think. 'The court's in your ball, Buster,' I muttered.

He was so incensed by the impropriety of my behaviour and so busy bawling me out that, on our way to the door, he led me into the Gents by mistake. 'Do you honestly expect him to burgle Moss Bros at this hour?' I said crossly. Fortunately the photographer was more amenable and agreed to go back to Highgate and change into a dinner jacket.

Traditionalism on the whole seems to be making a comeback, because one was also amazed by the number of debs presents. Ironically ever since Queen Charlotte's Ball was scrapped in 1976, they seem to have multiplied in their hundreds. According to Peter Townend, for the Rose Ball which took place later in the week, and which has now replaced Queen Charlotte's as the traditional debs' blast-off, they had sold a staggering 1,400 tickets at £17.50 a throw.

Just as the motor mechanics and the rich husbands of the Golden Eagles spent all evening thrusting cards into breast pockets, so the debs' Mums have stickers printed with their daughters' and their own names and addresses, and could be seen at the Caledonian Ball trying to get them into the diaries of as many other mothers giving parties as possible. Good contacts is the name of the ball game, and if you can do it in a flush of self-congratulation because you're raising money for the underprivileged, so much the better.

One of the more attractive things about the Caledonian Ball was that it had occasional flashes of silence like Macaulay's conversation. The band actually stopped for five minutes between dances. Unfortunately, most of the men were so tall that talking was rather like being in a basement trying to overhear conversation in the flat above. The floor was absolutely packed out during the Scottish dances, but deserted during the fox-trots and waltzes.

Now they were all pouring on to the floor for Hamilton House, muttering 'First you set to your partner, then to the man next to him', under their breath like children trying to recite tables before a maths lesson.

Seen from the gallery, the dancing was beautiful: great waves of scarlet, black and white, all shifting like the sea, now there were pockets of violent activity, now a wheel turning as an eight went round with their hands joined in the centre, now a pocket of stillness. It was erotic too, the way the men clasped the girls hands with both hands and drew them close as they swung them round – suddenly I wanted to play mixed doublets, but was still worried about my orange elbows.

At the end they all stamped and whistled and shouted for more like a Bob Dylan concert. One man stamped so hard, his foot went through the floor like Rumplestiltskin, so the band played again, and then again.

'Your grandfather when he was your age used to get through three collars a night,' said a dowager disapprovingly to a wilting youth.

Despite such energy, no one except our table seemed to be drinking alcohol. Back and forth staggered the waiters, carrrying three jugs of orange squash in one hand, three jugs of lemon in the other: Kia-Ora – it's the reel thing. The upper classes drink less because they don't need confidence boosters like the middle classes, and because they're tight with money. Perhaps the Scottish upper classes are even tighter.

'I was on the way to the bar to buy a bottle,' explained one ginless wonder, 'but fortunately a reel began, so I was saved in the nick of time. At the Highland Ball in January,' he confessed, 'where the drink is included in the ticket, everyone drinks like fishes.'

It was the same tale in the Ladies' lavatory.

'None of them tip,' sighed the attendant, philo-

135

sophically eating an orange. 'But they're much better behaved than they were a few years ago. One year more than a hundred of them lost their tickets, and were all shrieking for their coats at the same time.'

On the hangers were enough huskies to furnish every trip to the Antarctic since Captain Scott's. Nearby the same little girl in spectacles sat slowly combing her hair, looking sadly at her empty programme. Two girls were mending gashes in each other's dresses, and saying what a *pig* Jeremy was.

Beauties were wiping sweat off their faces and necks with paper handkerchiefs, and tossing them, not showing a trace of make-up, into an already overflowing plastic dustbin. All were scarlet in the face. Perhaps that's why Burns said his love was like a Red Red Rose.

Back at our table now, well lubricated with our whisky, Anglo-Scottish relations had improved dramatically except for my husband who was beginning to slide under the table. Two couples from our party had even ventured on to the floor. One girl returned instantly like a screw shot out of the Hoover.

'They take it horribly seriously,' she muttered. 'Men kept hissing "teapot" and "figgaruveight", through their teeth at me, and signalling, "We can't have *her* in our team" with their eyebrows.'

Charlie Carter, however, who used to play cricket for Somerset and who has such dazzling good looks that all the Scottish wives were dying to teach him the steps, was soon getting the hang of things and bounding round like a kangaroo.

'The Duke of Atholl looks just like Bernie Winters,' I said.

'Oh steady on,' said the Duke's agent nervously. 'I say, Johnnie, do you think the Duke looks like Bertie Winters?'

The only really hideous fashion on the floor was a dinner jacket, waistcoat and kilt all in the same red and black tartan with a red face and red hair to match – not unlike a tin of shortbread. I wasn't wild either about a ginger kilt with a ginger shawl worn over one shoulder like a drying-up cloth.

'He's a chieftain,' said one of the wives. 'Probably Irish,' she added disapprovingly.

Halfway through the evening, one of the giants in our party tempted me on to the floor. At first it was a nightmare. They toss you about like pass-the-parcel, although no one bothers to undo your string. Nor have I had to concentrate so hard since I went to a bingo hall, but after a few moments I forgot my inhibitions and my da-glo elbows, and began to enjoy myself.

Unfortnately I kept getting distracted by some stunning man glimpsed through a gap, and sidling down the row to have a gawp, and missing my turn. But with infinite forebearance, the giants in our party set me in the right direction. In their size and gentleness, they reminded me of great sturdy cobs, ideal to learn to ride on, who always slow down when you loose your stirrups, and wait nudging you with a friendly pink nose when you fall off.

Back at the table, I spoke to the Chairman of the Ball, another magnolia-skinned beauty with a penetrating voice. They expected to make about £3,000 for Scottish charities, she said.

'Terribly sorry about the fuss over the photographer.'

'He had to go all the way to Highgate to change,' I said reprovingly. It might have been Africa for all she knew.

'Oh well,' she said, brightening, 'I expect he'll get it back on corsts. That's my husband over there,' she added.

'Frightfully good-looking,' I said.

'And *fryte*-fly busy,' she said. 'He's an equerry to the Queen. We so enjoy your amusing articles in *The Sunday Telegraph*.'

People were now circling the floor doing the Blue Danube, any minute the band might lauch into 'Tay for Two'. We all piled back on to the floor for the last reel. Another floorboard gave way, everyone fell down it, one of the giants lost a silver buckle off his shoe.

At three-thirty, we staggered upstairs, almost asphyxiated by an old mushroom stench like dressing-up boxes. It must have been all those pints of sweat curling up in the tails and doublets for another year – so different from the white deodorized armpits of the Golden Eagles, and the Brut of motor traders.

Outside an innocent cerulean sky hung over the green fountain of the plane trees, and we thankfully breathed in a heavenly smell of lilac, dust, approaching rain, and the soapy scent of a thousand hawthorn trees.

'Can't think how anyone can live in London,' said a shattered young man. 'Pace is far too hot for me. Are you coming to the Game Conservancy Ball tomorrow, Fiona?'

'Yes,' said Fiona, who was easing her aching feet in totally flat ballet shoes, 'and the Rose Ball on Thursday.'

My poor husband, who had not enjoyed himself, had sunk into deeper and deeper gloom, and refused to take to the floor even once. As Monty once remarked to a friend of his who was introduced to him as a veteran of Anzio: 'Not my show, I'm afraid.'

The last straw, the next day, was that he'd lost one of Moss Bros's white ties, and the cat had slept all night on the discarded tail coat, so it had to be returned to Moss Bros covered in tabby fur. But perhaps this may set a new fashion for the motor traders, and instead of ox-blood and kingfisher blue, they'll roll up next year in tortoiseshell and marmalade – tails from the unexpected.

Swallows and amazons

It was Hen Night in Wandsworth on Wednesday. And I now know all about sisterhood. Apart from the joy of spending an evening with 200 women, there was the added incentive of two male strippers, called Sailor and Jack the Lad, assorted drag artists, chicken and chips and a free drink for only £4. 'Hen nights is very, very popular,' warned the manager of the pub beforehand, 'so get there early.'

Certainly when I rolled up 20 minutes before opening time, the queue outside the Horseshoes went halfway down the street. Nervously I attached myself to a chattering group of married women.

'What did Kev say when you said you was going to a strip?' asked one blonde.

'He said, tch,' said her friend.

At seven o'clock, flashing lights were turned on, and in we trooped, jostling, cackling, exuberant with anticipation. The front runners bagged the best tables round the richly red carpeted stage. On the scarlet flocked walls, double bridles and snaffles gleaming in the rosy light, looked suspiciously like instruments of sexual torture.

Muscular henchmen with broad shoulders, incredibly slim waists and jutting bums whizzed about fixing recording equipment, and nearly gouging out one's eyes with coathanger hooks, as they carried in glittering armfuls of sequinned dresses. One Greek God had so many swallows tattooed on his arms, it was a migration every time he passed.

The women were now queueing up for their free drink. Apart from a hard core of old cockney charladies who never took off their coats, the standard of female talent was staggeringly high.

'Men never bother on stag nights,' said the manager. 'But the ladies always dress up to the nines for an 'en night.'

Most glamorous of all and at least seven feet tall from her rhubarb-pink, backcombed hair to her seven-inch heels was a drag queen called Rusty, who lounged against the bar in black lace slashed to the groin, and rapaciously eyed the Greek God covered in swallows.

All the front seats were taken, so I edged into a lone chair beside a party of sekketries, who gazed into space and were obviously determined to make their free drink last all night. One pretty girl, who ate so many crisps you felt she'd crunch at the touch, said she felt very nervous about the strippers. She wished she hadn't come, because her boyfriend felt so 'frettened'.

To my right was a much jollier bunch of Wandsworth stalwarts in leather coats called Doreen, Mary, Mary, Treena, Margaret and Jean. 'Your first 'en night,' they said incredulously. 'You *will* enjoy it.'

Without the inhibiting presence of men, a fantastic cameraderie was building up.

There was a burst of music, and Rusty teetered on to the stage. 'Any girls not been to an 'en night before?' he drawled in his sepulchral baritone. A handful of women cautiously raised their hands. 'Well, 'ands up the virgins then.'

Two tables in front, a goaty-looking blonde shot up both her hands, to cackles of mirth from her friends.

The microphone gave an ear-splitting screech.

'That's nice,' smirked Rusty, as the Greek God bounded on to the stage to adjust it, 'this young man's coming to play with my nobs' (more shrieks of mirth).

After a few sexist jokes, Rusty introduced his 'very good friend, Norman Cable', another drag queen with ginger curls.

'Nice to see smiling faces,' said Norman, his lascivious

140

Molly Parkin eyes roving over the audience. 'Left all the bastards at 'ome, 'ave you?'

A great cheer went up. He then launched into a string of anti-male jokes, so filthy but funny that even the nearby sekketries stopped munching crisps and let out the occasional nervous giggle.

After a particularly blue crack, there was a commotion, and three charladies waddled to the door, chuntering furiously, demanding to be let out.

'What's up with them?' I asked.

'Got the wrong day,' explained Doreen, Mary and Mary. 'They thought it was an Irish night.'

Rusty now shimmered on in peacock-blue sequins, and announced the imminent approach of Sailor, the first stripper. The excitement was not so much sexual as the feverish anticipation of children on Christmas Eve.

The group of probation officers and social workers in the front row looked very apprehensive. There was a roll of drums. One of the social workers turned green. 'I know he's going to wave it in my face,' she squeaked and bolted out to the loo.

Clutching my bag like a chastity belt, I took her seat. Fortunately, frenzied smoking had reduced the visiblity to about three feet.

'I want you all to put your hands together for fabulous Sailor,' screamed Rusty, going completely over the top like Kermit.

Next moment, a plump young man with rosy cheeks, wearing a white sailor suit and a little sailor hat erupted into the room in a frenzy of jolliness, rather like Percy Grainger in the Delius film. Pulling one of the social workers to her feet, he rotated his pelvis against her, then gathered up a greyhaired woman in a spotted dress, and carried her screaming delightedly round the room. Casting her aside, he seized the reluctant hand of another social worker and pressed her until she'd removed his little hat.

He then bounded across the tables, sending typists

diving under their chairs, and now, horrors, he was advancing like the pantomime cat down the front row again. Rushing up to a pretty probation officer on my right, he thrust her hand down his trousers. She gave a gasp, then giggled, and drew out a red lollipop. With shaking hands, I just managed to undo one button and was presented with an orange lollipop. Lil from Balham, however, who was on my left, was livid, when after undoing three buttons, she was only rewarded with a green one.

'I 'ate lime flavour,' she said indignantly.

A blue-rinsed pensioner was now briskly removing his trousers, like a nanny stripping a tired child. Gym shoes came off next, followed by his shirt, to reveal a charging elephant tattooed all over his chest and he was down to the Union Jack pants.

'Get them off,' yelled the crowd.

He did, but underneath, was another pair of Union Jack pants, and then another, and then another, driving the crowd to a frenzy.

Suddenly he turned his back, and whisked his pants down to half-mast to reveal one heavily lashed eye tattooed on each cheek. The room collapsed in hysterical laughter. The lights dimmed, the drums rolled. For a second, he stood totally naked then he scampered off to wild applause.

'I prefer the Scarlet Pimpernel,' said Lil. ''E does flame throwing as well.'

In the queue for the loo, momumental boasting was going on. 'His winkle weren't nearly as big as my Norman's,' said a hoary old Cockney loudly. 'Nor as big as my Stan's neither,' said her friend. 'I shall tell Stan, then he won't feel so frettened.'

'And Anna Raeburn claims size is immaterial,' sighed a social worker.

After such excitement, we fell on our chicken and chips. It was my luck to be accosted by apparently the only feminist in the room.

'Don't you realize what a big thing it is for women,' she said earnestly, 'to have a night out away from their husbands. Don't you get a wonderful feeling of sisterhood?'

Seeing four large Bloody Marys lined up for me by Doreen, Mary and Mary, I said I did, and sidled off to talk to Sailor, who was now propping up the bar. He was a nice young man with the sort of sweet smile adored by mothers-in-law. We'd been a lovely, warm audience, he said, but then 'en nights were always more appreciative than cock and 'en nights.

'You can go as far as you like with just ladies,' he added. 'It's only when their old men come too, they get scared to laugh, and you have to tone down your act.'

How did he do that? Oh, he let the men pick out the lollipops.

Drag artist followed drag artist, the music grew louder, noses shone, Carmen curls drooped. Visibility was down to two feet now. On every table was a forest of glasses. The bar takings must have been stupendous. The evening was due to end at eleven, and it was now five to, with still no sign of the second stripper, Jack the Lad. The audience were getting restless, worrying what their husbands would say.

I took refuge against the bar with Balham Lil. But instead of Jack the Lad, we got yet another drag artist, Danny O'Dell, who was, mercifully, extremely funny. 'I love those beautiful clothes,' sighed Lil, as off came his silver lurex shirt, leaving massive red yellow and green plus-fourteens underneath. He then very slowly unearthed from them, a cat's tail, a gherkin, a feather duster, a tickling stick, a fox fur, a rubber cockerel, a vast cucumber, and copious other sexual aids.

'So predictable,' said the Feminist scornfully.

He was drawing out a nine-foot pink rubber snake, when my minicab driver arrived to collect me. One glance at the stage and the audience, and the happy smile froze on his face. He fled like Actaeon into the night.

143

Finally the drums rolled even more thunderously, and on came Jack the Lad, who turned out to be the Greek God, covered in swallows, who'd been humping equipment, now wearing a black silk shirt, green trousers, and high black boots.

'Good old Barbara,' screamed a group of sekketries, as he selected an eager middle-aged woman from their ranks and kissed her with such dumper-like force, I thought he'd pull her teeth out. After a scamper round the tables, he made the mistake of asking the Feminist to undo one of his shirt buttons. With one bound, she was on him, whipping off his shirt (you half expected a flock of swallows to fly out) and scrabbling frantically at his trousers and pants.

'I only asked for one button,' he hissed, recoiling in horror. 'Don't mess me up, you'll ruin my act.'

Radiant with self-importance, she returned to her party. 'The big phoney! You could tell how threatened he felt.'

'Strippers is very shy people,' said Balham Lil reprovingly.

Jack was now down to a black satin jockstrap, rather like a Jane Austen reticule. One had to confess, he was wonderfully constructed. As the lights dimmed, he lit three flaming torches and ran them over his bronzed sweating chest and thighs, before bravely swallowing them. A smell of singeing hung on the air. The audience, now whipped up to a frenzy, were standing on tables and stamping their feet.

'Off, off, off,' they screamed.

Obediently Jack the Lad draped himself in a blue towel, and whipped off his final defence. Then as a codpiece de resistance, he rotated his member round and round at a great speed like an English setter's tail. Then, even more brilliant, he turned his back on us, and went on rotating through his legs. A quick frontal whirl, back went the towel, and it was all over. I embraced Doreen, Mary and Mary and Co, and vowed to meet at the next

144

Hen Night. Outside a row of husbands stood patiently waiting on the pavement.

''spect they're 'oping for some side effects,' said Lil, going cackling into the night. It had been a marvellous evening. Happily I motored home. Planning to write a stirring tale about Sister Hood and her band of merry hens.

Men, women and
other close relations

Roasting Spare Rib

Recently I had a letter from the Cambridge Union asking me to take part in a debate on feminism. A lady from *Spare Rib* had evidently agreed to propose the motion, and when asked whom her magazine regarded as its greatest enemy, had unhesitatingly replied that it was me. Being a rotten speaker, and a coward, I refused the Union's invitation. As Public Enemy Number One, however, I thought I ought to look at a few back numbers of *Spare Rib* – which is celebrating its hundredth issue this month – to see what it's been up to.

The early numbers back in 1973 were grisly enough, being obsessed with the usual below-the-belt subjects such as rape, abortion, contraception, the curse, and dealing with them in a totally humourless way. One contributor, for example, wrote that she knows of women 'who can't wear the coil because their periods are beyond the help of two sanitary towels including VAT'.

And how the magazine detested men! A reader wrote in saying how much she enjoyed flying kites: 'such a marvellous escape from the boredom of males.' She had made her first kite thirty years ago, when on honeymoon with a gouty husband. The editorial staff were also enraged by a doctor who dared to suggest that women live longer because they keep nimble doing lots of housework. A poor, newly widowed woman was also branded as sexist because she wrote to *The Times* saying how she missed male company and conversation. Later in the same issue, there was a review of *Watership Down*, complaining that it was too male-dominated. 'Why do the Does only dig warrens and breed?'

The magazine also had an unnerving tendency to refer

to women collectively as 'sisters', or else coyly just by their Christian names, reminding me of a friend who once suggested that 'Rosy-fingered Dawn' sounded like three o'clock in a lesbian night club.

But in mitigation, there were some good if not very jolly features: on wife-battering, exploited Asian women, the terror of getting into the clutches of a National Health psychiatrist, and the appallingly restricted life led by women with young children in high-rise blocks.

The women's movement itself seemed rather fun in the early seventies. There are thrilling accounts of American feminists dressing up as red witches and disrupting male conferences, and even kidnapping two editors of a porn magazine. On one occasion they effected a Spaghetti House siege of *Ladies' Home Journal*, and by leaping for the throat of the male editor, terrorized him into commissioning an eight-page supplement for 10,000 dollars. But as I waded through more recent issues, the revolution seemed to become less fun, and the magazine's mood sourer and more virulently anti-male.

The attitude to children makes one's flesh creep. One feminist mother wrote that she was worried about going out to work and leaving her child with a less vigilant baby-minder. Her daughter, she said, already played happily with cars and garages, as well as dolls, but what about reading aloud? Would the baby-minder be sure to skip over the pages about Daddies and concentrate on the fact that women can use electric drills? (Perhaps she should divert the child's attention to the ads about vibrators.)

Another mother gives an account of taking her child to the theatre to see Beryl and the Perils. The little girl was terrified by the broomsticks outside the door, because school (oh sexist villain) had taught her that witches were nasty people. The child's view can hardly have been changed when the witches rushed on screaming: 'Mucus of bride, spit of spinster, lip of lesbian, mother's milk!'

Even more chilling is a taped dialogue between an

eleven-year-old daughter who's seen her mother through several affaires with women, a nervous breakdown, and finally joining a lesbian socialist feminist group.

'I know it's essential for you to be a Lesbian,' the child says, 'but you've never influenced me, I have lots of ideas about socialism, and I'm definitely very anti-sexist.'

She knows, she goes on, that her mother wouldn't mind her getting sexually involved with anyone, 'as long as it wasn't a conservative sexist male'. (At eleven – dear God.)

Sons of feminists fare even worse. The extreme fringe believe it's wrong to like not only men but also little boys. Many of them refuse to have a child in case – horrors! – they might produce a baby boy, who might one day turn into a full-grown enemy. (Oh for the days of King Herod.) The editorial columns even suggest a diet which is more likely to produce a girl than a boy baby, and they're very interested in a drug which emasculates men. Actually, it's called alcohol.

Great emphasis is placed on making men pull their weight domestically, and women having 'an equal share of the man's money without having to pay for it in love and kisses'. One contributor said she felt furious when her two sons 'appeared fascinated by soldiers and toughness'. Her husband, she added, did housework, and looked after the boys. 'But the fact that they don't oppress me is countered by the fear that they might.'

On the other hand the magazine has the temerity to publish fiction about a lesbian bemoaning an affaire that's broken up after twenty years: 'I can see things in the right perspective now,' says the abandoned woman sadly. 'Does it really matter who did the cooking or the washing up, or the ironing, I know that it mattered at the time. But oh what fools we were to let it eat into our once happy union.' Spare Rib would lynch any wife who said that to a husband who'd slacked on the housework.

And what really irritates one is the total irrationality of

151

the magazine. One moment it's ranting on about male clubs which exclude women, the next urging women to take up youth club work, and to press for all-girls evenings and dances which exclude men. There's also a hilarious account of a feminist rally in Majorca:

'We had a conference in Palma on woman and our bodies, and wouldn't let men in because we were showing how to use specula (instruments for spreading the vaginal walls, and examing the cervix). Many women bought specula, and rushed round the main square that night clacking them.' Bizet's *Carwomen* perhaps.

Equally illogical is a piece about Big and Beautiful (the Fatties' Lib faction) represented by Nancy of *Spare Tyre* (is there a sub-branch called *Inner Tubing?*). Nancy is livid with clothing manufacturers for not making fashion-able clothes in larger sizes. She knows quite well that the committed feminist rejects fashion because it puts money in the pockets of wicked capitalists, but why should not our big sisters have the opportunity to reject it too? They could always try Benjamin Edginton.

And despite all the protestations about sisterhood, if they come across a woman they disapprove of, they simply de-sex her. 'As for the Mrs Thatchers of this world', writes a contributor, 'they're just men.'

As I have already said this week *Spare Rib* is celebrating its hundredth issue – and it's a corker. 'The one thing wrong with S.R.,' grumbles a reader, 'is that you don't *blame* men enough.' Well, it's not through want of trying. To kick off there's a splendid interview with someone called Kate Monster *(sic)*:

'I rummaged round Edinburgh and found a lot of Scottish Lesbians, who got very drunk and laughed a lot,' (little did she realize perhaps that she'd stumbled on a Regimental Reunion of the Black Watch), 'and we rab-bited on about how different it would be if women loved each other, and men would get out of the way.'

There's also a piece on the five hundred women raped

in Soweto, and another inevitably entitled 'China – rough brown paper for periods', and another on Karate for the Disabled, complete with photographs, in which a woman in a wheelchair learns to 'kick her assailant with her orthopaedic shoe, and strike at his kidneys with her crutch'.

Pride of place however is given to an interview with Tony Benn, who after Jill Tweedie's panegyric in *The Guardian* recently is fast ousting Jane Fonda as the Sisters' Sweetheart.

Neither of the *Spare Rib* interviewers, nor Mr Benn, listen very hard to the questions or pick anyone up on the answers. *Spare Rib* claims predictably that all women are oppressed and all men the oppressors. Wedgie counters somewhat that surely lady landowners and bankers are not oppressed, and might there not be rich women even who oppress men. *Spare Rib* ignores this and picks him up on not being more supportive to the sisterhood. Ah, replies Wedgie, they had not heard him tearing a strip off the steel workers in Wales the other day because they wanted nudes not only on page three, but on pages one and two as well.

Finally there's even an anti-male poem:

As they snicker their way through some joke at the
     bar, I
Sit and wonder from afar, at
Fifteen years of married bliss, and
Most of it spent with him
On the piss.

Not very stirring stuff – next month they should print my marching song:

The Grand old Dyke of York,
She loathed ten thousand men.
She marched them up to the bedroom door,
Then went to bed with her 'friend'.

153

As an added centenary celebration this week, *Spare Rib* is holding an exhibition at the Cockpit, Princeton Street, London WC1 (rather a sexist venue). But you won't see me there, I'm going to bed in a pink baby-doll nightie with twelve Barbara Cartland novels. A socialist had pointed out recently that Miss Cartland's books are in fact female pornography.

And yet, and yet, one is left with a feeling of sadness that *Spare Rib*, having championed the underbitch for so long, and provided a life line for many unhappy women, should antagonize so many others by its enmity and bitterness. Obviously there are thousands of loving, responsible lesbian mothers, and feminists who have affection for men as well as little boys, and equally thousands of women who are badly treated by their men. But as Kate Millet pointed out in the seventeenth issue of *Spare Rib* back in 1973, the revolution will be won by love not hate.

The day of the wimp

Recently I complained that men were becoming so wet and emasculated by the women's movement that the only place left to see male virility was on the rugger field. This caused such howls of rage and disbelief that I decided to do some deeper research into the subject.

'Why are men getting so wet?' I asked an elderly dog-walking friend.

'Chickens,' she boomed. 'If they eat all those capons stuffed with female hormones, you can't expect them to be very masculine.' And fixing a well-known local flasher with a withering look, she sent him fleeing back into a nearby blackthorn copse.

I turned for illumination to the newspapers. Suddenly they hardly seemed to be mentioning men at all. Over Christmas it had been rape, rape, rape. Now it was interminable questionnaires in which girls under twenty-five stressed that careers were infinitely more important than caresses. Page after page was devoted to assertive, achieving women, who rose at six, leapt on to exercise bicycles and then rushed off to run vast pharmaceutical empires single handed.

'Woman is born free, but is everywhere in chains', raged a *Guardian* headline, as though the entire female sex were either indulging in bondage jamborees or suffering a fate worse than oppressed black slaves in the eighteenth century.

Everywhere, women seemed to be taking over men's traditional roles. There was even a case of a scout-master sacked for having an affaire with a *lady* cub-leader. One had only to look at Mrs Thatcher and then at her Cabinet, or at Elizabeth Taylor, bursting with vitality, and then at the ravaged, self-pitying wreck that was Burton, to see which sex has the energy.

More significant perhaps, if you gaze up at the sky the next clear night you will see the planet Mars glittering menacingly in the constellation Virgo. Women are on the warpath.

Driving through Knightsbridge last week I was overtaken by a short-haired girl in a Hunter Super. On the back was a sticker saying 'Men have only two faults: everything they do and everything they say'. No wonder the entire male sex is suffering from battle fatigue and feeling not unlike the declining Romans as the Barbarian hordes swept into town.

I first became conscious of declining male virility about two years ago when a very handsome QC asked me out to lunch and then stood me up without a word of apology. A cloud no bigger than a man's handbag perhaps, but gradually I realized fewer and fewer men were bothering to chat me up at parties. Maybe it was because I had reached middle age but asking around I found younger and infinitely more desirable girls were experiencing the same phenomenon.

I was tremendously comforted when I came across a passage in a novel called *The Serial* by Cyra McFadden, which is a marvellously funny send-up of American trendies in the late seventies:

'Just a few years ago,' Kate, the bewildered heroine recalls, 'the husbands in her peer group had stroked her bare spine when she wore her backless dress to parties and told her she figured spectacularly in their dream lives. Now they were liberated, all the men who had propositioned her, had long since apologized and told her they really really respected her as a person. And, of course, she wouldn't dream of being seen dead as a sex object.'

Any kind of sexual desire has suddenly become terribly frowned on. The Pope inveighs against lust – even within marriage – and in America they've even started fining wolfwhistlers. At this rate you'll soon be whipped off to the electric chair for sending valentine cards.

In a Barnes gifte shoppe, a mug shaped vaguely like a woman's torso and inscribed with the words 'It is company policy to work hard or wear a tight sweater' has been marked down from a fiver to 99 pence and shoved to the back of the window.

Even *Cosmopolitan*, once the temple of sexual Sybaritism, has gone stuffy: 'Thumbs down,' wrote last month's issue, 'to Doncaster Rugby League Club, on the streaker's band wagon with its ad for 42-inch-chested girl for half-time entertainment.'

If you remove lures, you will gradually eliminate lust. In similar vein I was rung up by a feminist student the other day. She was writing a book on sexual harassment in the office.

'You worked in an office once didn't you, Jill?' she asked earnestly. 'Did men ever harass you?'

'Yes,' I replied. 'But not nearly enough.'

There was a long and terrible pause.

The trouble with the feminist movement is that they cannot recognize an ally when they see one. My dear husband, although sometimes a shade bossy, or as the Americans would say 'overly directive', is the kindest, most considerate and understanding man where women are concerned. He merely reserves the right to laugh at them (and men too) when he chooses. As a result he is constantly attacked by the Women in Publishing group for being a sexist pig.

I wish they had been there after the last office party when he alone got in at 7.30 a.m. to tidy up the shambles and hoover the boardroom because all the women in the office considered it beneath them.

Offices must be like minefields at the moment. It is the aggressive over-reaction of women that men seem to find so debilitating.

'You can shout at a male colleague,' said a designer

157

friend, 'and he's forgotten it in two minutes. Women sulk for weeks.'

I'm rather surprised they haven't introduced PMT rotas on the office notice-board, along with the holiday list: 'Watch out for fireworks from Fiona on the fifth, and Jennifer's likely to be crotchety around the seventh.'

I was relieved when I discovered the same phenomenon of angry women and cringing retreating men was even more acute in America.

'If women were furious, men were to blame,' claimed a recent copy of *Playboy*. 'For the first time since biblical days women were having sex without guilt, but men were having guilt without sex. Men were supposed to be vulnerable, either you cried all over a woman's shirt on the first date or you were an insensitive lout – the day of the wimp was upon us.'

It is significant that a year or two ago, American women voted a neurotic wimp like Woody Allen the sexiest man in the USA – a far cry indeed from Rhett Butler.

You can see the wimp here in the spate of television plays about ineffectual men, Charles Ryder dripping about looking pained, or the ghastly *Alexa*, in which the wimpish young schoolmaster not only pulled his wife's best friend, in between grumbling, but also had to confess to his wife immediately afterwards.

The wimp tends to be more prevalent in the 30–55 age group because his confidence seems most shattered by the feminist movement. Also to the loss of an empire and failure to hold our own economically against other industrial nations, are added the fear of unemployment, and the pressures of the consumer society, which bombard him on television with macho images, while simultaneously eroding his role as a provider, and filling his wife and children with dissatisfaction if they cannot carry on acquiring.

Nor can he claim the sanctity of the minority group. It's frightfully bad form these days to make jokes about

gays, Jews, blacks, Irish, women, the young and the aged
– so the only target left is the white heterosexual
middle-aged male.

Young men, as we shall see later, seem much more
adaptable to the feminist onslaught, and homosexuals,
who used to be very twitchy a few years ago, are now far
more together. They have been able to voice their grie-
vances through Gay Lib. So many have come out of the
closet they are almost a majority group, and, because
there's a strong feminine element in their characters, they
seem far less threatened by the women's movement.

Not so the heterosexual male, who probably in the
early part of his marriage ruled the roost like Chanticleer.
Suddenly his wife goes back to work and he is made to
feel terribly guilty if he's not doing far more in the house
and rushing back home in the middle of board meetings
to experience what *The Guardian* would call 'the joys
and frustrations of parenting'. If his wife is more successful than he is, he may have pressure put on him to give up
work altogether and look after the house and children.
There is nothing wrong in this, but he will have to be a
very strong man if he doesn't feel his masculinity eroded.
One Putney house-husband suddenly turned up at parties
wearing a dress.

Fear is the parent of cruelty and the nastiest backlash is
the closet wimp who hides his insecurity in ferocious
bullying. One unemployed man I know lived with a very
pretty girl who supported him by working in public
relations. She was very good at her job and frequently
had to work late. So her lover started telling her quite
untruthfully that her breath smelt and that he didn't
know how she dared lunch with clients or approach
anyone at press parties. He thus created the perfect
modern chastity belt by making her terrified of even
talking to men, let alone looking for someone else.

Men have probably become even more uncertain and
wimpish as women become more aggressive in relation-
ships.

'If Charlie comes home drunk and picky,' said one friend, 'I wait until he's asleep and then sock him. He wakes up with a yelp, and I say, "you've had a bad dream, sweetheart", so he falls asleep and I sock him again.'

Another man I know snapped at his girlfriend because she spent too long on the telephone, so she threw an entire Irish stew over him, then hurled his trousers out of the window. By the time he'd put on his jacket and underpants and run down four flights of stairs, his trousers had been stolen and she'd locked him out, so he had to pretend to be jogging home.

Nor has the obsession with jogging helped anyone's sex drive. When I was at school we were sent on cross-country runs to douse our libido and keep our minds off the vicar and the under-gardener. Now the whole nation's at it, or guilty that it isn't. Every party you go to, men are standing around with their legs apart to ease the jogger's chafe, wearing a fresh coat of sweat and far too busy capping each other's stories about how far they've run that evening to bother talking to women. A miss is certainly not as good as a mile.

It hasn't helped that we've moved from an age of hedonism to one of asceticism. No one eats or drinks any more. To reassure myself the species still existed, I lunched out with two former hell-raisers last week. The first was on a diet, and consumed only a rare steak and his own nails because he'd just given up smoking. The other ordered a Bloody Mary, melon and a tomato salad. Only the other day, the vastly reduced husband of a health food fanatic rang up and in a tearful whisper begged me to smuggle him in a loaf of Mother's Pride when we came down for the weekend.

Dinner parties aren't as fun as they used to be either. No one gets abandoned or wildly indiscreet because they're all sloshing back Perrier. That rules out passes. No Englishman is likely to pounce on a girl if his stomach is empty of Dutch courage and filled up with bubbles like an Aero bar.

Nor am I remotely encouraged by the information that

160

Warren Beatty, allegedly the greatest stud in the business, doesn't smoke, seldom drinks, and dined last Christmas on a salad of beetroot and kale, washed down with celery juice. (I distrust Americans anyway. They may be abstemious about food, alcohol and nicotine but, while staying in Los Angeles recently, a friend said the local doctor turned up to attend her chicken-poxed children, stripped to the waist to reveal a conker brown suntan, coked up to the eyeballs, and smoking a joint.)

But to return to those middle-aged wimps. You see almost more insecurity in the ones on the loose. Often raw from a disastrous marriage, they seem to thrive on rejection.

'For six months he pestered me to leave my husband and move in with him,' said a girlfriend bitterly. 'Then the moment I said yes, you couldn't see him for dust.'

'Men are all over you,' said one divorcee, 'as long as you appear to be going out with lots of people. The moment you show them they're the only one, they're off.'

The unacceptable face of capitulation, I suppose. Perhaps because all the sexual lures are fast being removed, men only fancy women when they're in flight.

'Men are so spoilt,' said another friend, 'they expect you to pick them up for a date in your car, and at the end of the evening after they've been absolutely useless in bed they expect you to drive them home.'

This is the way the whirl ends — not with a bang, with a wimp.

Wimps get away with it, of course, because there's such a dearth of spare men in London. The moment a marriage breaks up, they're snapped up like the big houses along Putney Common. On the rare occasions I meet a glamorous single man at a party, I tend to look at him not with lust but with the eye of a recruiting officer, in the hope I might enlist him for one of my numerous single girlfriends.

One writer was kicked out because he wasn't earning enough. 'For the first fortnight,' he said, 'I restored my self-respect by pulling everything in sight. But gradually the laundry got me down. Every time I ran out I bought more shirts, pants and socks. Then it was early-closing day and as I had an interview the next day I was forced to wash some things overnight. But they weren't dry in the morning. I drove to the interview in a polo-neck sweater and draped a pair of pants and socks on the windscreen heater hoping they'd dry on the way. I nearly killed myself because the windows kept misting up. After that I gave up and moved in with a girl.'

From the evidence I can glean it's not just the wimps who are feeling threatened by women at the moment. I lunched, for example, with a very attractive middle-aged man the other day, who had been married recently for the second time. He promptly ordered a dozen snails.

'Then hopefully,' he added, his voice booming round a transfixed restaurant, 'I can sleep by myself tonight.'

'But you've only been married six weeks,' I protested.

'I know, and I can't stand her. She's so bossy and demanding. She won't let me put the paper down on the sofa, in case it leaves newsprint on the new covers.'

To back up my theory of declining male virility, I talked to Dr Terence Solomon, who runs a gynaecological practice in the West End, and specializes in sex problems. One of the most acute problems he has to deal with is lack of desire. He had a case that week of a 39-year-old advertising man and his 32-year-old barrister wife. Although she was most attractive, and the husband was surrounded by beautiful women at work, he had no desire to have sex with anyone.

'My wife's so aggressive,' he complained, 'she questions everything I say. I am never in a state of mental cosiness.'

'That is the crux of the problem,' said Dr Solomon. 'Women can pick their own sexuality, but if they want sex with a male, they will have to make things cosy for him.'

Another increasing problem, he said, was impotence:

'We are dealing with the first generation of women liberated by the Pill. They can play havoc with their partners if they boss or, even worse, laugh at them.'

It is interesting that the two most popular women in England today have wildly contrasting appeals. The first is the gentle, ultra-feminine Princess Diana, who chose looking after children as a career, the one pastime the women's movement claim is boring and demeaning. The second is Pamela Stephenson, beautiful, bawdy, and more than capable of looking after herself. Happiest wearing men's suits, she claims that men today are attracted to very strong women.

Admittedly the best party I have been to recently was when I dressed very butchly in black boots and trousers, a white silk shirt and a black tie. Suddenly all sorts of wimps who had never shown a flicker of interest before started prowling round me.

'I can just see you with a whip,' sighed one wistfully.

Equally my secretary went out the other night dressed like a head waiter, and came home starry eyed at 11.30 next morning, saying she'd had the most wonderful time of her life. But are women dressed like men so irresistible to today's male because he is narcissistic and likes a mirror image, or because he feels less threatened with a sort of chap, or because he is getting more feminine? I suspect the latter. Where girls once invaded men's boutiques, now females' clothes-shops swarm with men diving through a forest of bras to try on girls' trousers. My secretary's boyfriends keep annexing her shirts.

'I only fancy Adam Ant,' sighed my ten-year-old daughter, 'when he's got his make-up on.'

One notices too that all the boys have Jeremy Ironed their hair flat, while the girls are making themselves as tall as possible coaxing their spiky hair upwards. I gather they use contraceptive paste for the purpose – perhaps it's the only need they have for it.

On holiday, according to a courier friend, men grumble

less than women, and ask for more blow-driers. In Bologna last year, a taxi driver told me a marvellous story about a recent conference of English marketing men who completely fused the hotel's power system, all blow-drying their hair before going out on the town.

And how about the dating patterns of the young? An American survey showed that young men still initiate dates in 90 per cent of the cases, thus 'setting themselves up for rejection at every stage of the game'.

I notice boys today tend to slip their telephone numbers into the back pocket of a girl's trousers, in the hope that she will take up the option if she wants to. Most young couples seem to go Dutch after the first date – which means you can afford to go to more interesting places and the boy has the reassurance that the girl is going out for his company not his bank balance. My secretary paid for dinner on Saturday, her boyfriend cooked Sunday lunch.

As men retreat, however, girls become more predatory.

'We were at Battersea Town Hall,' said a comely blonde, 'dancing to Dicky Hart and the Pace-makers, when this girl from another group took a shine to the man I was with. Every time we got up to dance she came over and asked if she could dance with us. He was far too weak to say no.'

Young people also seem better at adapting to what has been called today's chameleon world of androgyny. A girl at a party the other day was paying a lot of attention to a pretty youth.

'I'm afraid I'm gay,' he said.

'Good,' she said. 'I only like boys who've been to bed with other boys.'

My niece, when she was thirteen, was so in love with a nervous youth that when she had a birthday party she put place cards inscribed with his name on both sides of her at supper.

Girls also have to appear tough to keep their end up with other women. A pretty schoolmistress I know had a row with her boyfriend. When he turned up next day at the school to apologize bearing a huge bunch of roses, she snatched the flowers and, aware that the entire staff room was watching, rammed them straight into the dustbin, only to retrieve them after everyone had gone home.

On the whole though, the young seem more relaxed in their attitudes:

'May I bring my flat-mate to lunch?' asked my niece the other day. I envisaged some fuzzy-haired female geography graduate but she turned up with an extraordinarly good-looking and charming South African boy. When I started looking all eager and match-making, she explained it was completely platonic as they both had other people. In my day I'd have gone into a decline of desire and embarrassment at living in such close proximity to someone of such beauty.

Evidently though in mixed flats they all run around with no clothes on and no one thinks anything about it. Surely, too, boys who live with girls from such a young age (and sisters aren't the same) will have a much better understanding of women's problems generally and also feel less threatened by the demands of the feminists because everyone mucks in with the housework.

My nephew, who is at Bristol, lives in a mixed flat with a boy and three girls.

'We leave the washing up for three days,' he explained. 'Then someone does it and gets terribly self-righteous and spends the next three days telling everyone. No, I don't think anyone's ever cleaned the kitchen floor.'

Cooking is another communal pastime.

'Simon and I start and Ella who's a brilliant cook usually has to finish off. We tried to cook a chicken for a dinner party and boiled it for three hours in water with some onions. It was absolutely disgusting until Ella came back and transformed it into Chicken Maryland in about ten minutes.

'We tidy up if we have a dinner party, or parents are imminent. We had a friend staying who kept belching and making the most disgusting smells, so when someone's mother turned up unexpectedly, the girls locked him in the bathroom for two hours.'

As he is very personable, my nephew admitted that girls did ring him up.

'But only for a chat, they don't actually ask you out. Although there's one awful girl who reads engineering who never says anything but just stands at my shoulder when we do practical work, breathing very heavily.'

But, although the young may have got their sex lives more together, they are bound to be affected by the endless feminist propaganda, telling them how trifling and inadequate men are. At least in my day, we enjoyed dreaming about Mr Right coming along looking like Rhett Butler. Now, according to the women's movement, all a young girl can look forward to is Mr Can't-Put-A-Foot-Right.

However, all is not lost. In New York, which is invariably five years ahead of London, the feminist movement has gone off the boil. Demoralized by the increasing wimpishness and dearth of spare men, American women have suddenly decided it is all right to be a sex object again.

'Women,' according to *Playboy*, 'have realized something precious in the male has been driven into hiding. It is time to welcome him back, a man who respected women, but who didn't pander to them, who was capable of lust without apology, who above all revelled in his maleness.'

If real men are making a comeback in New York, with any luck they should reach London by the late 1980s. I shall fill in the time writing a novel about a broiler-suited feminist lady having a passionate affair with Rhett Butler, called *Gone with the Wimp*.

The last of the summer whine

I was really longing for the school holidays this summer. As I'd just finished two books, I decided to have a break and devote myself to the family. I wasn't even worried that my living-in secretary was going on holiday. A charming Cornish temporary nanny was coming to help out and answer the telephone, and I had a small BBC script to write to keep my hand in.

I was also stung by my husband's accusation that by locking myself in my study for nearly a year, I'd lost all touch with reality. What better way to re-find it than to be a housewife and mother for a few weeks.

First week of the holiday: Felix breaks up. Very peaceful except for delightful crew of workmen who have been in the house for two months, who are now rebuilding the conservatory. In addition to the endless cups of coffee and incessant incoming telephone calls about Superfilla and undercoat, this means that my plants are all on the terrace dying of sunstroke, that the dogs bark frenziedly two hundred times a day whenever the workmen let themselves in and out, and I cannot type topless in the garden.

Had also forgotten that the next week I have two signing sessions, three wireless and two television programmes to do, and about twenty-five people to stay. Feel I am grasping reality by the nettle.

Week two – Tuesday: Both children broken up and already at each other's throats. House like a sauna – discover we cannot turn off central heating.

Wednesday: Ring Gas Board about central heating. Emily has little friend for the night. Screams issue from drawing room. Punch-up because Emily feels little friend as house guest should select television programme. Felix does not. My husband, Leo, returns in ratty mood because little friend occupying his dressing room, and likely to depart with one cufflink and a cricket sock in place of a moccasin and Miss Piggy pants.

Thursday: To avoid repeat of yesterday's punch-up, Felix buys television advertised in local paper for £5, and collects it from nearby council estate in minicab. Roaring snowstorm on all three channels as workmen spend all day trying to adjust set. House still like a sauna – old and new television sit side by side in drawing room; perhaps they'll mate and produce family of little portables.

Friday: Cornish temp arrives. Children seem to like her. As usual I treat her as house guest, and, abandoning all work, rush around saying 'Don't overdo it', and cooking three meals a day.

Week three – Monday: Felix having graduated from jumble sales to auctions this holiday, returns with tape-recorder with prolapse and four wirelesses with only two registers: off and *fortissimo*. Reason for slow progress of workmen is that they are constantly deployed to tinker with auction spoils. Reason for slow progress of Cornish temp is that she is constantly distracted by matchless beauty of chief builder.

Tuesday: Temperature and central heating rocket. Emily changes four times a day using my room as dirty-clothes basket. Adam and the Ants blare out against circular saw; oh, the hols are alive with the sound of music. Felix says he's bored and decides to plaster his room. Weakly agree for sake of two hours' peace on BBC script. Telephone rings ten times. Find Felix's room in chaos, plaster and

168

paint everywhere, particularly over new shirt and jeans. Cook lunch, children squabble vociferously and grind Rubik cubes looking far from cherubic. Feel like Trappist monk just emerged from silent order after twenty-five years. Blinding headache nudging skull. Forestalled by Cornish temp who retires to bed with blinding headache.

She rises after two hours and asks if she can go for a little drive in our ailing motor. Returns three hours later, as I am ringing the police, saying accelerator pedal fell off. Leo walks in saying place is Absolute Shambles, and why am I cooking children's supper?

Wednesday: Return from BBC to find temp doubled up, saying she must see doctor. Torn between passionate sympathy for her – and myself. Kitchen looks as though bomb has hit it. Saucepan-demonium. Emily asks if she can make toffee from recipe which says 'Mother must stand by for ten minutes while sugar boils'. Mother refuses shrilly. Emily makes martyred telephone call, then says she has been invited down road to make toffee by more understanding mother. Feel a heel. Cornish temp admitted to casualty ward of local hospital. Leo returns complaining blue jersey vanished. Hastily retrieve from dog basket.

Thursday: Take minicab to hospital to deliver clothes, grapes, etc. to Cornish temp. Utterly fail to charm bootfaced nurse, who says don't put anything in temp's locker as she's being moved to Surgical this afternoon.

Back home Felix says he's bored, can he paint the bookshelf in my study? Quail at prospect of two hundred books joining chaos on study floor. Weakly agree he can paint Emily's bookcase, but not to paint carpet. Go into Emily's room five minutes later to find books all over carpet. Look outside just in time to see bookcase collapsing on lawn like camel. Grinning workmen say it's a write-off. Ensuing row between me and Felix heard by entire street. Go out to lunch leaving workmen to baby-sit.

See fellow prep-school parent in restaurant, who asks fondly after Felix. Deeply shocked by my reply. Say, he's never wanted to murder *his* children. Suggests Felix and I spend relaxing afternoon at British Museum. Suspect we may find calmer type of Mummy there.

Return home. Darling Felix has made my bed, and all the dogs' baskets. Filled with love. While immersed in incomprehensible missive from Gas Board, absent-mindedly agree he can have 12-bore for his birthday.

Emily tells me a joke then asks why do I always say 'Ha, Ha, Ha, that's very funny', and not mean it, and can she have a packet of Frazzles?

Gas Board arrive unexpectedly, scratch heads over tropical central heating, and say only way to adjust it is at pump concealed in hollow behind newly painted and plastered kitchen wall. Ask faintly if they are quite sure. Gas Board says 99 per cent sure, definitely. I look the other way, as with tears pouring down his handsome face, chief builder bashes down wall which took him weeks to paint and plaster. We all peer into chasm. No pump to be seen. Builder and I display admirable restraint. Gas Board show total lack of contrition and saying 'that's the trouble wiv old houses', depart leaving us to clear up devastation.

Friday: Cornish temp returns from hospital feeling like death.

Saturday: Temp still ill. Leo insists we find instant replacement. Ex-nanny of friend agrees very sweetly to come down from Derbyshire to help us out of crisis. Cornish temp asks if she can stay on for second week as house guest. Feebly agree, but as four house guests due shortly, wonder where they'll all sleep.

Sunday: Judge horse show in Hertfordshire. Learn on grapevine that organizer would have preferred me to wear a dress. Wish I'd turned up in twenty yards of turquoise tulle covered in sequins. Return home to find Cornish temp sufficiently recovered to go for drink with handsome builder, and Leo, who has cooked lunch for twelve people single-handed, understandably resting on his labours.

Find Felix's bedroom where new temp is to sleep still in state of mid-plaster with every drawer tipped out over floor. I am frantically hoovering and changing sheets, when Leo walks in and hits roof. How can new temp get true sense of crisis, he roars, if I make house look like furniture polish ad? Snap back that she will hardly relish sheets lined with Jaffacake crumbs, chewed crayon, and cat fur. Just get room habitable in time for her, when puppy re-creates sense of crisis by disembowelling stuffed Noddy all over carpet. Emily sleeps in our bed, Felix sleeps in camp bed in our room. Dogs have fleas and scratch all night to accompaniment of holidaying neighbours' burglar alarm.

Week four – Monday: Return from television programme to find washing-up machine top-heavy with workmen's coffee cups, and both temps sitting in garden worshipping handsome builder, who is even browner than my plants. Cook lunch. Felix explains that new temp doesn't feel in charge because of presence of old temp. Open £40 Gas Board bill for not locating pump. Upstairs Emily has been trying on all my shoes and make-up, and the puppy has been trying on counterpane. Walk on Common to regain temper. Senior dog has small fight. Puppy rolls joyously in unspeakable fox droppings, and rushing home bounces over fastidious house guest who has just arrived plus friend with parrot and dog. Try to water dying plants but find workmen have borrowed watering can to mix cement.

With two temps, four house guests, three children, one husband, three dogs, four cats, and a hundred croaking plants to cherish, feel like too-small piece of butter trying to spread itself over too many boiled potatoes.

Tuesday: School friend arrives to stay with Felix, whose mood improves dramatically. Both depart to auction, and return with several cameras for £5, at least one of which they say, with commendable optimism, works. As Felix has friend, Emily asks can Daisy stay the night? Felix says he can't stand Daisy. Row follows inevitable course.

Wednesday: Escape on to Common for some peace. Charming Australian house guest pounds past on jog, looking like jolly green giant. He changes his clothes more often than Emily, then hands them to us to wash. Children indulge in 'Emily's borrowed my bike – Well, Felix borrowed my ear-phones' argument. Take them to High Street for haircuts. Forced to walk because Cornish temp disappears for another little drive in motor to take chocolates as thank-you present to hospital. Returns three hours later – am about to murder her when she very sweetly presents me with single red rose.

Thursday: Taking down Royal Wedding flag nearly go through balcony above drawing room. On examination, workmen say ceiling is rotten – probably because I've hit it so often this summer – and will cost £1,000 to repair. Cornish temporary departs. Motor finally expires. Felix's school friend departs. Hostilities between Felix and Emily now concentrated in kitchen as workmen bashing down drawing-room ceiling. Entire house covered in white dust.

Emily says she's never been More Bored in her Life. Suggestion that she does my tax returns, or my last six months' expenses, met with stony stare. Walk dogs in blazing sun to escape from central heating, return at 2.45 to find second temp sitting in garden admiring handsome builder. Asks if they can slip away for twenty minutes until pubs close. They return two and a half hours later, by which time the telephone has rung twenty-five times. Contemplate black comedy entitled *A la Research de Temps perdu*. Felix says I should have bought him that

172

12-bore after all. Don't trust myself to speak to temp, depute Felix to tell her to defrost fridge.

Leo returns twenty minutes later to find every kitchen surface covered by melting fish fingers, moribund sausages, and half-inch-full mugs of French dressing, and asks why we live in such a tip. Scream at him. Try to pour drink, saying furiously: 'People have been drinking our drink, there was half a bottle here this morning.' Temper not improved when Leo points out there is still half a bottle, I have merely failed to unscrew the top.

Friday: Workmen bash down more ceiling, and finally finish conservatory. Puppy has pink-eye, I have pink eye, Leo nearly has black eye. Find him replacing my plants in conservatory, including plumbago on top shelf. Point out through gritted teeth that plumbago grows upwards. Leo drops plumbago downwards, scattering John Innes over newly polished floor. Frank exchange of four-letter words unsuitably enjoyed by children.

Later Leo catches me adding garlic and an Oxo cube to casserole of hearts I'm cooking for dogs. Deny hotly that I love dogs more than him, but add that sometimes they are nicer to me. Leo adds darkly that they wouldn't be if they could talk.

Go and sulk on Common. New orange moon rises between the sycamores. Wish on it that newest book may be bestseller, then appalled by venal egocentricity of wish. What about Leo's torn Achilles tendon, the children's collective Common Entrances, and the puppy's pink-eye. Remember friend of my father saying all men get bad-tempered during summer holiday because wives too tired for sex. Rush home and upstairs to find Leo asleep.

Discover temp washing handsome builder's jeans. Why does such altruism irritate me to death, when she is already washing and ironing four shirts a day for Australian house guest? Felix goes to country to stay with school friend. Hostilities blissfully suspended.

Week five – Monday: Woken at dawn by police helicopter searching for missing local child. Rush guiltily into Emily's room to find her sleeping peacefully. Ring up Felix as early as possible. School friend's mother says he's fine. She's most impressed because he's just come indoors to read. Her son, she adds, never opens a book. What's he reading? I ask in a glow of pride. *Exchange & Mart*, comes the reply.

Tuesday: Felix back from country having had a 'triffic' time. Emily says she wants to live in the country and have a pony. Hostilities resume more clamorously than ever. Leo says I am not strict enough.

Wednesday: Leo takes the children, plus little friend of Emily's, to cricket. Returns ashen beneath suntan, and sends children to bed with no supper. They've quarrelled all day, he says, have I any idea what they're like? Decline to point out too forcefully that I have been discovering for several weeks. Discuss moving to country. Leo has nightmare about Emily quarrelling with the Queen.

Thursday: Wrestle with BBC script, now dangerously overdue. Telephone rings twenty times, ending with fellow-writer, saying his children never quarrel, and mine do because as a career woman I'm a rotten mother.

Replace telephone and sob for ten minutes, then ring up cousin with four adorable, biddable children, and heavenly house in country dripping with ponies and swimming pools. Before I have time to beg her to find me a house like hers, she says her children have driven her crazy fighting the entire holidays.

'Even Beattie?' I say incredulously.

'Beattie's the worst. She was poison all the way through Charlotte's birthday party, and when I ticked her off afterwards, she blamed it all on God. Said she'd asked Him to make her specially good, but he'd done nothing about it.'

174

Ring off feeling ridiculously cheered up. Hug children and decide not to live in country. Don't even worry that much when cat is sick over evening paper, and handsome builder comes in and says as they've nearly finished in the drawing room, they'll be taking all the carpets up tomorrow in order to paint the skirting boards.

Mind the step

As the divorce rate rockets, and more and more people remarry, the pattern of family Christmas is changing. In America, according to the *Daily Mail*, it's reached a state when Father Christmases in department stores are instructed not to ask a child how Mummy and Daddy are, because he or she may not be living with them, and long explanations hold up the queue. Instead they are told to ask 'How are the Folks?' which is more neutral.

Back in England, a headmistress who wanted to fill the hall for the school nativity play, urged all the children to bring their parents. Whereupon a small boy raised his hand and asked: 'How many parents may one bring?'

In the old days, Christmas dinner was typified by the Pater-familias at the head of the table, flanked by two rows of admiring rosy-cheeked children with Mama up the other end. Today's father, on the other hand, is surrounded by a host of semi-familiars: stepchildren, stepgrannies, sister-in-law plus two children born out of wedlock, mother-in-law plus new husband, his own children who normally live with his first wife, not to mention his current wife and children. Perhaps it should be called Xmas, because there's a mass of Exes about.

Christmas with its compulsory goodwill and loving kindness tends to make people behave badly anyway. With the added rivalry of siblings, in-laws and steps, it's not surprising that all over England families are already revving up to fight the third world war.

It takes just a Christmas card from an ex-mother-in-law, forgetting perhaps deliberately to include the new husband, to trigger off hostilities well into the new year. Or a second wife, acutely conscious of working her fingers to the bone, will be carrying a swimming bath full of turkey fat from the oven to the sink, when the first wife rings up to wish her children a Merry Christmas.

Children, who usually get on with the offspring of their parents' other marriages, are bewildered by such animosity. Their main problem is divided loyalties. Will their mother who hasn't remarried be desperately lonely, if they spend Christmas with their father who has?

What is infinitely more tragic is when neither side wants the child. A girl who works in a local shop told me she hadn't been home for Christmas for fifteen years. When she was nine her mother walked out on Christmas Eve, leaving her to bring up her five-year-old brother, and look after her father. Four years later, just before Christmas, her father suddenly announced he was marrying again the next day.

'When I came downstairs the morning after the wedding, my stepmother was cooking Christmas dinner and told me to keep out of the way because it was *her* kitchen now. On Boxing Day she threw me out because I reminded her too much of my Mum.

'Next year, I'd tracked down my Mum and went to spend Christmas with her. She'd married again and got a new baby. They were both all over it. I got jealous, there was a row. Next morning, my stepfather told me to get out. He said I was upsetting my Mum, but admitted he didn't like me round because I reminded him of my Dad.'

The root of the problem with the steps – as with in-laws – is jealousy. Conflict comes particularly at Christmas, when husbands or wives in a spirit of goodwill try to heal breaches that the other half may not want healed.

Virginia Ironside, the Agony Aunt on *Woman* magazine, told me the crisis she most often has to deal with at Christmas is when a second husband arranges to deliver some presents to the children of his first marriage. To give him courage, he gets tanked up beforehand, and, armed with parcels slightly damp from the bar counter, arrives at his first wife's house, and has a few more drinks. In the relief of reconciliation, he loses all sense of time, and doesn't get home until midnight – to find his second wife in hysterics, hitting out left, right and Santa.

The first year I was married, I spent Christmas Eve in floods of tears. I was in Yorkshire staying with my in-laws, and had a lovely time, until I delved into the Christmas box to wrap up my presents and found a sheet of paper covered in mistletoe on which was written a tender Christmas message to my husband from his first wife.

Terrible rows can also flare up because the remarried mother is so anxious not to neglect her children that she ignores her new husband.

'She won't put a lock on the bedroom door,' complained one husband, 'so our sex life is a shambles. Last Christmas when we were living together, her children came in at five o'clock in the morning to open their stockings. After that they burrowed under the bedclothes, and the little girl finally emerged demanding: "Why isn't Jonathan's willie as big as Daddy's?"'

For the sake of the children, some people conceal their hostility under a veneer of sophistication. One Lancashire millionaire insists on all his three ex-wives coming to stay for Christmas, plus their new husbands and children. The first wife does the cooking. 'It's highly civilized,' she said bitterly, 'except for piranha fish in the finger bowls and no one meeting anyone else's eyes.'

Evidently the third wife blotted her copy book by running off with the butler, and wasn't allowed back to the Christmas family reunion until she'd jettisoned him and run off with a barrister whom her first husband considered was the right class.

I suppose there must be an element of masochistic excitement in competing with three other wives. It would certainly give added incentive to the pre-Christmas crash diet.

Again for the sake of the children of his first marriage, a sculptor friend who's made a very happy second marriage, insists on asking his first wife for a drink on Christmas Day.

'The pattern is horribly the same,' he explained. 'This barrage balloon in a jet-black wig marches in, promptly tells me I've put on a lot of weight, and hasn't my beard gone grey? Through gritted teeth, I then offer her a glass of champagne. Whereupon (making a mental note to demand more maintenance) she cries: "Champagne! We *are* going up in the world."

'Then she comments on the new curtains (which are actually six years old) and some pictures she and I were supposed to have bought together in the old days. Then when I stump out in a rage, she turns to my present wife, saying sympathetically, "I'm *so* sorry he hasn't got any easier".

'The other thing that irritates me to death is the way she tries to seduce my children by my second wife, "buying" their affection with ludicrously expensive presents then ringing up two days later to say how surprised she is they haven't written to thank her yet. If I had a dog, she'd try and seduce it with liqueur chocdrops.'

But suddenly the kaleidoscope shifts, because it must be hell for the first wife. I try to imagine what I'd feel if my husband fell madly in love with and married some much younger and more beautiful girl with pots of money, and the children suddenly wanted to spend Christmas with them, because it was more fun and the pickings were better. I'd find it impossibly difficult not to poison them against the new wife.

It should be remembered, however, that although the step problem is more acute today, it is not new. St Joseph was a stepfather – and it must have been pretty denting for his macho to have to succeed God as a first husband. How did Joseph feel in the stable with the animals all bowing down and the shepherds freaking out over his miraculous new stepchild? Did he accuse the Wise Men of trying to 'buy' Jesus' affection? Was he jealous later in life, when the boy grew up and was always banging on about his real father in heaven? Perhaps Joseph was canonized because he fulfilled a difficult role with such compassion and dignity.

One tends to think Joseph wasn't jealous because he was an old man, and therefore past such passion. But in my experience, stepgrandparents tend to behave more pettily than step-parents.

'My mother-in-law,' explained one husband, 'liked my wife's first husband much better than me probably because he's richer and she could bully him. The old witch can't fly her broomstick any more, so every Christmas I have to drive two hundred miles to fetch her. She then spends her time picking on my children from my first marriage, and pointing out how slow they are at Scrabble, compared with my stepchildren, at whom she smiles with deep understanding sympathy every time I raise my voice.'

Another girlfriend had an even worse time last Christmas with two grannies at permanent yule loggerheads.

'In one narrow four-storey house, we had my present husband, our two children, three children from my first marriage, and my mother and my mother-in-law, who'd both just been widowed. The children got on like a dream, it was just the two widows permanently battling to be the most popular granny.

'When we were opening our presents, my mother insisted our youngest daughter should open the largest present first. It turned out to be a vast doll my mother had made herself, having collected fluff from other people's spin-driers all year in order to stuff it.

'The moment my mother-in-law saw it, she screeched: "Oh look, children, it's just like Mary! You remember Mary, the big doll I made for you two years ago?"

'They also fought continually to be the most helpful grandmother, following me round saying "What shall I do?" then drowning their sorrows over another bucket of whisky and soda, and forgetting to do it. In the end I made a list of tasks and came down next morning to the unedifying sight of two grey-haired, dressing-gowned ladies fighting over the kettle. In despair I laced both their coffee heavily with Valium and came back half an hour later to find them hanging round each others' necks.'

Stepfathers are traditionally more easygoing than stepmothers, but as they get older they seem to get considerably more crotchety and difficult. One stockbroker, not famed for his tact, was staying for Christmas with his mother-in-law and her new husband Algie who is in his seventies.

'Just as we were going into Christmas dinner,' the stockbroker told me, 'Algie made some crack about a friend of mine. I shut him up, said I wasn't going to have my friends insulted. Seeing Algie was looking a bit bleak, I offered to carve the turkey for him, and took over. Twenty minutes after we'd sat down to dinner, we all realized Algie wasn't there. He'd gone to bed in a sulk, and refused to come down again.'

Another aspect of the new 'multiple family', as the Americans call it, is that it creates havoc with the generation gap. A fifty-year-old man may suddenly acquire a colicky baby as a stepsister, or a father achieve a grandchild older than his youngest child.

One woman friend has a very pretty stepdaughter who, perhaps because her father left home when she was a baby, is heavily into older men. Last year the stepdaughter brought her new lover to stay for Christmas.

'He turned out to be an aging satyr with coaxed forward grey curls,' said my woman friend, 'about five years older than me. When he asked where he was sleeping, I tried to be very modern and said I'd put them both in Henry's dressing room. Whereupon he looked dreadfully shocked, and said there was nothing like that between him and my stepdaughter, so I had to apologize like mad, and rush off and iron some sheets and make up a bed on the study sofa. The ridiculous thing was we heard them commuting all night between Henry's dressing room and the study. I suppose he regarded us as potential in-laws, and wanted to appear respectable. But he wrecked his prospects, when Henry wandered absent-mindedly into his dressing room to get some cufflinks, and found him blow drying his grey curls.'

One of the few advantages of the multiple family is that, in some areas, attitudes are more relaxed. The stepmother tends to get less beady about a stepson who turns up wearing eye-liner and with bright blue hair, or a stepdaughter's bearded vegan boyfriend who farts all the way through the Queen's speech, because subconsciously she doesn't mind if her stepchildren look frightful, or shack up with unsuitable people. Whereas a real mother would have a heart attack.

But often it's a stepparental indifference and lack of interest that makes stepchildren behave so badly. I am still haunted by the saga of the girl from the local shop. At fourteen, after both parents had rejected her at Christmas, she moved to London, got into a bad set, was soon mainlining, and ended up with two years in prison for peddling dope. Since then she has had three children, all three of whom she left with their fathers because she didn't want them caught between the cross-fires of separated parents. Only now, after years of psychoanalysis and heroic effort has she managed to get her life together.

Hers is an extreme case, but despite the battles, the good thing about Christmas is that it does give us the chance to try again, to see someone else's point of view, to realize that a husband's love will grow rather than decrease if one is sometimes prepared to share it, to behave like St Joseph rather than Cinderella's wicked stepmother.

For surely one of the greatest compliments was paid by a little girl to her father's second wife: 'I'm terribly terribly lucky,' she confided to a friend at school, 'because I've got a spare Mummy.'

A happy Christmas to you all, but do mind the step.

Middle-aged wife's tale

My first piece for *The Sunday Times* appeared thirteen years ago in the colour magazine. Entitled 'A Young Wife's Tale', it described the joys and problems of our first years of marriage.

Since then marriage has been under siege, leaving the stage littered with bodies. Women's Lib has come and not gone. Wives, we are told, are leaving their husbands in droves because of the rawness of their deal. Divorce, a hideous spectre at the wedding feast, stoppeth one in three like the Ancient Mariner.

Watching the three-legged race at my daughter's sports day last year, I was struck by how much the couples symbolized today's two-career marriage. Some stumbled past supporting one another, others fell over and packed it in in a flood of tears, some of the speediest runners were hopelessly impeded by slow partners, yet a few, obviously after a lot of practice, had managed to achieve a smooth and steady progression.

A friend depressed me immeasurably the other day by bitterly quoting Margaret Drabble's claim that one cannot have a career, children and a husband – something has to go, usually the husband. On reflection, I decided this was defeatist and, if you were lucky enough to have the right husband, all three were possible.

People often wonder how Mrs Thatcher got to the top while looking after a husband and two children. I found out at a party at Downing Street earlier this year. Arriving twenty minutes after it was due to start, I found only Denis and a couple from the GLC occupying the huge double drawing room. Mrs Thatcher, explained Denis, had been coping with the miners and would be down soon. I was just thinking how nice he was, and how infinitely less of an ass than his public image suggests, when in swept Mrs T. looking ravishing in dark blue frills, wafting scent from her bath-warm body like regalia lilies at twilight. Instantly Denis turned to her, saying:

'Darling, how lovely to see you, and how marvellous you look.'

There was no question of the pride and delight in his voice, or the affection between them, and I realized what a tremendous support he must have been to her over the years.

Denis is a rarity. 'The majority of husbands,' said Balzac, 'remind me of an orangutan trying to play the violin.' Though not putting myself remotely in the same league as Mrs Thatcher, I too am lucky to be married to a rarity, a husband who picks up my every vibe, who senses when I'm getting overtired, and who, realizing there are times when writers must write, will calmly take over running the house and looking after the children.

Some things of course have had to go. Twelve years ago, Hunter Davies told me that when he, or his wife, Margaret Forster, were working on a book, they never went out in the evenings. I was appalled. In those days, my life was strung like a paper chain from party to party. Today, there are weeks on end when we hardly go out, seldom entertain, and spend all weekends at home, tidying up the mess I've made during the week, de-jungling the garden, or both simply working. Sadly one loses friends, but the real ones understand and wait for us to re-surface.

In the old days I tried, like Mrs Thatcher, to cook my husband's breakfast, but merely filled the house with the smell of charred toast. Better to marry and not to burn. Now I merely drop a multi-vitamin pill into a glass of water. Sometimes as a treat, I take it up to him in bed. I used to cook a two-course dinner in the evenings during the week, because I wanted to emphasize my cherishingly wifely role. Experience has taught me if I stop work at eight o'clock, he would much prefer an hour's chatter over a couple of drinks, and later baked beans eaten out of the tin.

We also turned our dining room into a second drawing room, so we can unwind in peace without being interrupted by double somersaults and shrill voices arguing over the relative merits of television programmes. A dressing room for Leo helped too, so he could escape from the flotsam of my clutter. Separate cars – albeit two bangers just able to limp through their MOT – also added to our marital harmony. No longer at 8.30 in the morning do I find the car gone, and six little girls frantic to be transported to school. Separate razors also reduced our squabbling dramatically.

But not separate beds. In a two-career marriage, it is all too easy to skip sex when you're both exhausted and under pressure. Only when you have it, do you realize how much you needed it, and what tension was caused by its lack. With my body, I thee worship, says the Prayer Book wisely, which means not only *revere* but *regularly attend*. Although, as a girlfriend who dotes on her husband remarked the other day: 'It is rather hard to worship Jamey some mornings when he wakes up smelling like a sewage farm: cigars, whisky, last night's curry, and the general dyspepsia of middle-aged stress.'

In a marriage as intense as ours, jealousy too is inevitable. Even today when I talk to my mother on the telephone for longer than five minutes, Leo starts banging pans, and, all the way down the wires from Brighton, I can hear my father irritably rustling *The Times*. I get sick with jealousy if I think Leo is interested in someone else. His methods are more direct. The other day, when I'd been talking to a man on the sofa for half an hour with all the absorption of sudden mutual attraction, in walked Leo with a plate of cut-up oranges, which he thrust under our noses saying: 'Half Time.'

With middle age too, one has less and less inclination to wander. The spring always unsettles me a little, but its such a hassle after an illicit lunch, rushing home, getting back into my old clothes, washing off my make-up and the scent behind my ears, so I'll look normal when Leo returns from work.

The children grow more watchful too, and have recently come up with middle stump questions like: 'Have you ever mated with anyone else but Daddy?'

My poor secretary was slightly nonplussed the other day, when (in the car, of course, where there's no direct eye-contact) one of them asked: 'How old were you when you had your first organism?'

At thirteen and ten, I have to confess they have reached most enchanting ages, lovely to talk to, incredibly kind and considerate, and – because they've had to be – very self-sufficient. They can get their own breakfasts, hoover if need be, go to the shops for me, do the vegetables, and best of all leave me alone with a hangover in the morning. One friend admitted the secret of her happy marriage was teaching both her children to iron their own clothes from the age of six.

Job's comforters assure me I'm living in halcyon days. You'll never get a wink of sleep, they warn me, once Emily starts going out with boys, and Felix is old enough to drive. I can't wait, he'll be able to drive me all over London and save a fortune in minicab bills.

If Leo and I row over the children it's principally because he has higher standards than I do, and detests any of us watching rubbish on television. Every week last summer, I, the children, my secretary, three dogs and four cats squeezed in a decadent row onto the sofa, and in the blazing afternoon sunshine, sat glued to the repeats of *Dallas* (which we hadn't been allowed to watch first time round) praying the 22 bus would get stuck on the bridge and Leo wouldn't get home in time to catch us.

Another reason marriage is under siege at the moment is that most couples have less money than they used to, which makes people very bad-tempered. Two years ago, when we were so seriously in debt that the bank urged us to sell our house, and I spent every day in the potting shed hiding from our creditors, Leo and I absolutely crucified each other. Raw with resentment, we seemed to be fighting every evening. Baked beans lose their charm when they're the only thing you can afford.

Happily things got better, and we both cheered up. As my daughter said to one of her little friends, who'd been bawled out by her workaholic father: 'Why don't you borrow my Daddy for a bit, he's got *so* much nicer since he changed his job.'

So many husbands have been forced to become workaholics to make ends meet or because they're terrified of losing their jobs, and as a result neglect their wives. Others have been laid off or got the sack, and, macho dented, slink around at home getting in the way. One has only to listen to the wifely acrimony in the fish queue: 'When I came in from work, he'd done sod all except the junior crossword, and leave splashes all over the sink. Hadn't even washed up the children's breakfast.'

Few things make women more bitter than not being supported as they were formerly accustomed. I know one girl who returned from her second honeymoon, opened her new husband's bank account for the first time, and promply packed her bags.

For others cumulative irritation not lack of money is the last straw. Two years ago, I met an enchanting girl at the races, only to be told the next day that she'd recently murdered her husband, plunging a carving knife into him because he'd asked her for the hundredth time whether the small forks went inside the big forks.

I've never taken the carving knife to Leo. But one evening during our financial crisis, I walked into the bedroom very proudly wearing a dark brown woollen nightie trimmed with white lace which I'd bought for twopence at a jumble sale, only to be told to take it off at once because I looked like a 'disgusting old friar'. Later that night when he was sleeping peacefully and I heard one of the dogs drinking out of his water mug, I merely laughed and turned over.

Leo is also keen on honesty in marriage, which, because I'm the more hopeless, usually boils down to a vigorous listing of my ineptitudes. Some days he comes home in a picky mood (usually because he's had to wait hours in the cold for the 22 bus) to find all the lights blazing. Having banged around upstairs, he comes into the kitchen demanding *why* I'm opening a tin of cat food, when there are already three gathering mould in the fridge, *why* I persist in putting knives the wrong way up in the washing up machine and putting crosses in sprouts which only makes them soggy, and *why* I don't let him do the potatoes because he does them so much quicker.

After a long pause, he asks me why I'm sulking, to which, through gritted teeth, I reply that I am not. Whereupon he points out the muscle going in my cheek, and suggests I must have the curse coming. He then progresses to the vegetable rack, and discovering the rotting spinach dripping dispiritedly onto the wrinkled carrots, demands why I waste money all the time.

At this point, I usually take the fight into the enemy camp, by pointing out the massive chunk his Wheeler's bill is taking out of our joint account, to be told sharply that we are not talking about *him* and why do I always fight dirty. I then retire and fight dirtier, by cleaning the bath with his flannel.

After twenty years, he has learnt to cater for my chronic disorganization. What rocks the boat are my occasional attempts at efficiency. As a result, this year we paid the minicab bill twice and the electricity bill three times. Leo also got two anonoymous valentines, date-stamped by the office, because I couldn't remember whether I'd posted the first one. Thinking I'd plan ahead when his father came to stay last week, I organized the shopping on Friday, telling him on Saturday morning, that all we lacked was some olive oil. Naturally he didn't believe me, and we ended up with twenty-four croissants,

6lb of broad beans, 3 lb of mushrooms, and two legs of pork.

Partly from a dread of getting into debt, and partly from laziness, I never get anything mended or done to the house. Consequently, Leo is forced to extremes. The other day I had a particularly difficult piece to finish, when an electrician arrived to fix the bathroom light string which, after months of it being so short we had to climb on to a chair to pull it on with our nails, had finally disappeared. The electrician was followed by a man to measure some carpets followed by a nice man delivering five massive cabinets to accommodate what is laughingly known as my filing, which completely blocked up the hall. Finally two undergraduates rolled up to remove the eight-foot-high toy cupboard, which Leo had decided was an eyesore on the top landing. Within an hour they had completed the task, leaving me in hysterics, and twelve years' accummulation of over-priced plastic and leaking board games all over the top floor.

Unwisely I telephoned Leo and screamed.

'I told you they were all coming,' he said.

'You didn't, you didn't.'

'I did, but you were, as usual, too wrapped up in yourself to listen.'

The middle stump again.

'Is Daddy going to divalse you?' asked my daughter as I came off the telephone. Leaving me to ponder gloomily who on earth would put up with me if he did. Besides I like sleeping on the left side of the bed, and who else would do my VA1 and tolerate a multi-vitamin pill for breakfast? I would also miss being married to the Escoffier of Putney. We may not bother much during the week, but at the weekend Leo does run up the most delicious food: sea trout with curried prawns, kipper pâté wrapped in bacon *en croûte*. He was once making a spinach tart when the mixer exploded coating the ceiling with a most attractive veneer of green purée, which remained there for eighteen months until we had the kitchen painted.

Which brings me to weight — not middle-aged spread exactly, since I weigh the same as I did the day I got married, but sadly the world has got thinner. Watching a clip of Real Madrid playing Eintrach Frankfurt in the sixties on television the other night, the players all looked as fat as butter compared with today's lithe demigods. It's bad enough making ends meet financially, but even worse trying to join the ends of one's waistband. The only answer is a nappy pin. The fiercest fights in our house in fact are over the custody of the last nappy pin. To keep the peace, I recently despatched my secretary to buy separate ones.

'Blue or pink?' asked our local chemist, who prides himself on being the fount of all Putney gossip.

'Both,' said my secretary.

'Don't tell me,' said the chemist, falling over the counter in his excitement, 'that Mrs Cooper's expecting twins!'

Over twenty years, though, we are gradually learning tolerance. Marriage — Margaret Drabble again — is a complex game of bargaining. I put up with Leo's ancient incontinent tabby cat, he grits his teeth when the puppy chews up his batting gloves. He was nice when I forgot to pack the sponge-bag recently, I was nice when his bonfire singed my new syringa bush. And if I'm sometimes incensed by his sense of fair play (nothing irritates me more at an international when he stands up and applauds a try scored by the other side), I am touched by his fierce loyalty. In his office drawer, he has a supply of postcards of Beachy Head. On the back of which, he writes, 'Why don't you go and jump off it?' to anyone he considers has been unkind to me.

But perhaps most precious of all in our marriage is the friendship, the sharing of experience, the hysterical private jokes that shake the bed, the post-mortems after parties, the luxury of having someone loving you despite spare tyres and crêpe on the thighs, the living in each other's heart, the haunting fear that one day one of you

190

must die. Will you still need me, will you still feed me when I'm sixty-four?

Flipping through my diaries for the last twelve years, I am shocked by the records of rows and the number of times I have written 'Leo and I are getting on horribly at the moment'. Yet looking back on our marriage, I only remember the happy times, as one's childhood always seemed filled with sunshine and buttercups.

One in three marriages breaking up is a chilling statistic, bringing appalling unhappiness to adults, and even worse to children. Surely couples should distinguish between a bad patch which may improve, and a total marital breakdown, and try a bit harder. From my diaries, there are half-a-dozen times when I thought of bolting. Thank God I didn't.

Every day when I walk my dogs at lunchtime, I meet a couple who must be in their late seventies, possibly eighties. She is a very pretty woman, and in summer wears a straw hat with yellow flowers. They walk hand in hand, slower than they did eight years ago, but they always seem to be laughing and delighting in each other's company. They have been married fifty years. That to me is achievement, a life work as great as painting the Sistine Chapel.

The pattern of flowers on the outside of my wedding ring is almost worn away, but inside as deep as ever is engraved: L.C. 7.10.61. J.S. I hope in thirty years, I shall be lucky enough to write a piece to celebrate my golden wedding called 'An Old Wive's Tale'.

THE END

JILLY COOPER TITLES AVAILABLE FROM CORGI BOOKS

WHILE EVERY EFFORT IS MADE TO KEEP PRICES LOW, IT IS SOMETIMES NECESSARY TO INCREASE PRICES AT SHORT NOTICE. CORGI BOOKS RESERVE THE RIGHT TO SHOW NEW RETAIL PRICES ON COVERS WHICH MAY DIFFER FROM THOSE PREVIOUSLY ADVERTISED IN THE TEXT OR ELSEWHERE.

THE PRICES SHOWN BELOW WERE CORRECT AT THE TIME OF GOING TO PRESS (JANUARY '84).

All these books are available at your bookshop or newsagent, or can be ordered direct from the publisher. Just tick the titles you want and fill in the form below.

CORGI BOOKS. Cash Sales Department, P.O. Box 11, Falmouth, Cornwall.

Please send cheque or postal order, no currency.

Please allow cost of book(s) plus the following for postage and packing:

U.K. Customers. Allow 45p for the first book, 20p for the second book and 14p for each additional book ordered, to a maximum charge of £1.63.

ˉ.F.P.O. and EIRE. Allow 45p for the first book, 20p for the second book plus 14p per copy for the next seven books, thereafter 8p per book.

OVERSEAS CUSTOMERS. Allow 75p for the first book and 21p per copy for each additional book.

NAME (block letters) —————————————————————————————

ADDRESS ——————————————————————————————————